THE EGO CONTINUUM II

One day [...] in yourself as much as I do!

Mark

THE EGO CONTINUUM II

NEXT GENERATION ACTIVE LEADERSHIP:

SELF-AWARENESS, LEADERSHIP BRAND, EFFECTIVE FEEDBACK DELIVERY AND **YOU**.

MARK ROBINSON

PEACH ELEPHANT PRESS

This book is designed to provide information that the author believes to be accurate on the subject matter it covers, and is written from the author's personal experience. In the text that follows, many people's and company's names and identifying characteristics have been changed, so far that any resemblance to actual persons, living or dead, events, companies or locales is entirely coincidental.

Any references to resources and materials produced by other entities are purely the author's own interpretation. The author does not imply an endorsement from any of the sources cited within this book.

ISBN 978-0-473-42796-2 (PAPERBACK)
ISBN 978-0-473-42799-3 (KINDLE)

THE EGO CONTINUUM is a registered trademark of Mark Robinson.

Copyright © 2018 by Mark Robinson
All rights reserved. This book or any portion thereof may not be reproduced or used in any manner whatsoever without the express written permission of the publisher or author except for the use of brief quotations in a book review.

First Printing, 2018

Peach Elephant Press
CreateNonFiction.com

*To my Mom and Dad, Ferne
and Malcolm Robinson.*

*I think about you both often
and it simply makes me smile.*

CONTENTS

acknowledgments   ix

introduction
A Deeper Lens on Leadership   1

one
What Does Being a Shitty Leader Really Mean   21

two
Shitty Leader Behaviours   27

three
Connecting Behaviours to Actions & Feelings   32

four
Don't Shoot The Messenger   48

five
Dealing with Shame   58

six
Recap of The Ego Continuum   64

seven
The Shadows You Cast   71

eight
Self-Awareness Awareness   78

nine
The How of Self-Awareness — 88

ten
The Frequency Leadership Matrix — 103

eleven
Explanation of Leadership Brand — 115

twelve
Building and Marketing — 123

thirteen
Recap & Creating Your Leadership Brand — 136

fourteen
Reviewing Effective Feedback Delivery — 140

fifteen
Why Delivery Matters — 145

sixteen
Dictatorship vs Democracy — 164

seventeen
Opinion vs Feedback — 170

eighteen
Your Ego Continuum — 181

nineteen
ROI: Exception Management & Time Savings — 190

twenty
Putting It All Together — 194

twenty-one
Leading Resistant Employees — 203

resources — 212

ACKNOWLEDGMENTS

To the Ego-Continuum Team! I couldn't — and wouldn't want to — do this without you.

- Pat Dunwoody
- Matt Cole
- Shari Coulter
- Victoria Morrison

To all the friends and family support. Thank you!

To my awesome children Alyssa and Alex. Love you!

To Esbe and Paul, thank you for being so supportive during this journey. I have learned so much. Third times a charm!

To my work colleagues who've spent hours listening to it all — thank you for your time, feedback and insights.

To the countless shitty leaders out there; past, present and future, a sincere thank you for shooting the messenger, blaming the messenger and eventually taking stock of what the messenger has to say. Your deflections, reflections and epiphanies have helped make this possible. Keep holding up that mirror; it works!

Much love to all.

INTRODUCTION

"No one makes you feel inferior without your consent."
— Eleanor Roosevelt

A Deeper Lens on Leadership

Someone once said to me, "You can't push water up a mountain!" Of course, this is very true. One might argue semantics; a dry-witted, sarcastic guy like me might talk about carrying the water up the mountain in a bucket. You can make attempts. But, cheeky or not, the reality is, at the end of the day, water naturally flows down the mountain. The top of the mountain offers only one direction of travel — down. That's where the water's journey starts.

With any type of change initiative, it is always best to start at the beginning. Obvious, yes? In the corporate world, that's top-level management: the top of the mountain.

In many cases, that means the shittiest of shitty leaders. If you try to start change initiatives at middle management, people will be stuck convincing those above them, who might be quite set in their ways, proud to admit change is required or just simply unaware or reluctant. Those top-tier shitty leaders require special attention, statistics, metrics, return on investment formulas and, sometimes, a great big wake-up call. In fairness, some of these executives may not have been on the receiving end of constructive feedback for decades, so any behaviours they've demonstrated may very well have become their status quo. How do you tell someone who has not received any constructive feedback since mullets were in fashion that they are unapproachable, unsupportive, or just a good old-fashioned bully?

If you've read our first book, you're already familiar with the concept of managing up. You also understand that by asking two specific questions to your direct reports, you will learn and demonstrate how to deliver feedback; customised and conveyed to them effectively. You know that it's not about you — it's about them.

When you need to manage up and deliver feedback to your manager, you simply do the same thing. Mention that you'd like to provide some constructive feedback and ask:

> Would they be open to it?
> How would they like to receive it?

Managing up can be a daunting task because your executive team might not always be open to it. If they are unwilling to engage in these discussions, it makes it much harder to change things for the better.

This is where we can help.

Most senior executives prefer facts and data. They like metrics. When reviewing your current culture, look at the following areas:

> How many members of staff have left in the last 12 months and why?

> Focus on your unwanted attrition. Those you wish had never left. Your strong performers. Why did they leave?
> How much rework do you and your teams have to do due to poor communications, lack of clarity or guidance, lack of plan or strategy, or simply those choosing not to follow process?

The cost of rework across the globe is staggering. If you told your senior executive team that billions are being wasted due to a disengaged workforce, would they be willing to listen?

There's only one way to find out.

WHAT IS LEADERSHIP?

If you're choosing not to lead from a place of humility and authenticity, then you're not really leading. Because, odds are, you're making it about you. It's not about you; it's about them. You will read this often in this book.

Many people confuse management with leadership. We manage processes, and we lead people. No one wants to be managed. The notion of being managed automatically sets our guard up. No one wants to manage, either — I mean, would you rather go to management training, or leadership training?

But here's the secret: training you to be an effective leader is a lot harder than training you to be an effective manager. The *only* way you can become an effective leader is by knowing who you are. Until you know yourself, you will struggle with what you're doing. You may immediately disagree. Many do.

But what if we know what we're writing about? What if one of your staff challenges you and doesn't like the way you've provided feedback? What are you going to do, tell them to shut up and do it anyway? Ignore?

Those are shitty leadership behaviours. That's perpetuating this very cycle. But how do you know when you're self-aware — and when you're not? Ask yourself, are you self-aware enough to know you're self-aware? More on this later.

STATS & METRICS

In our online research quest for data on disengagement in the workplace, we found that 75% of people cite their boss as the biggest cause of stress at work, yet 59% of workers with a poor manager don't leave. They might quit — emotionally, mentally, in every way but 'officially' — but they don't leave. They quit and stay. That's the beginning of a disengaged workforce, which costs businesses across the world a lot of money.

According to the Engagement Institute, the cost of rework in the US and Canada is between $450 and $550 billion annually. In Japan, it's $232 billion. In the UK, it's $65 billion.

That's the cost of rework. That's the cost of duplication. That's the cost of sick time. That's the cost of disengaged employees.

Why are your employees disengaged? Because they work for shitty leaders in some capacity. Bullying and harassment are impacting your employees and the bottom line. Constant bullying or the perception of bullying incites stress.

In 2017, 49% of US employees say culture influences their employee experience more than their physical environment (22%) or the technology they use to do their jobs (29%).

The top five stress symptoms causing missed work days are constant fatigue (29%); sleeplessness (26%); aches and pains (24%); high anxiety (23%) and weight gain (18%).

But you don't have to be an outright bully to be a shitty leader. You can do that simply by not caring or putting forth the perception of not caring. Did you know that only 21% of employees say their performance is managed in a way that motivates them to do outstanding work? 42% of employees believe their accomplishments go completely unnoticed. The same percentage feel that executive leaders do not contribute to positive company culture. 84% of employees believe praise should be given on a continuous year-round basis.

Think about how you deliver performance reviews. Once a year doesn't even remotely cut it when 84% of employees are looking for year-round, in-the-moment feedback. When was the last time you pulled someone aside and said, "Thank you for your contributions. Thank you for doing this."? Try it, and watch how people react. The second you say, "Hey, do you have a minute? I want to give you some feedback," people instantly think they've done something wrong.

That's part of this epidemic! I overheard a contact centre advisor on a call who was pulling out all the stops. He was articulate, caring, displayed the right level of empathy; it was just a great call. I wanted to tell him, so I walked over and said, "I just overheard you on that call and wanted to tell you it sounded great, well done. Keep doing that!" He looked utterly shocked. He didn't know how to respond, and it was clear that this type of feedback was uncommon, at least for this advisor. The employee's immediate reactions to positive feedback were shock and surprise. As a result, he felt uncomfortable.

I later found out it was a good news story that spread around the centre; nonetheless, leaders don't do this enough.

Perhaps this is part of the epidemic of shitty leaders? Perhaps this is an outcome where you keep making it about you?

Something is clearly not working. Our leaders are not contributing to positive company culture. And if we don't do something about it, the cycle will almost certainly continue. As the baby boomers continue into retirement and the millennials move into the workplace, these stats will compound. Those millennials will grow bitter and frustrated, being on the receiving end of all that shitty leadership, and that will just create a new generation of shitty leaders. People usually only mirror what they see, after all.

Shitty leadership creates workplace havoc through stress and anxiety. It contributes to staff disengaging and underperforming. It taints relationships and adds toxicity to the environment. It disables development and contributes to poor internal survey scores, as we've shared. It is the catalyst that determines whether your staff quit and leave, or quit and stay.

How can we change our behaviour? How can we change the corporate culture? Because when you have an engaged workforce, the numbers tell a different story. Look at the results of businesses that are engaged. A Gallup poll from 2017 found that highly engaged businesses have a 41% reduction in absenteeism, 21% greater profitability, 20% increase in sales, 17% increase in productivity, and a 10% increase in customer ratings.

Imagine the difference to your bottom line if you could get your staff engaged. The numbers are staggering; the metrics reveal it: the only reasonable thing to do at this point is to introduce new leadership styles and tools into the workplace.

Because we're facing an epidemic.

THE GLOBAL EPIDEMIC OF SHITTY LEADERSHIP

While we were in production for the first Ego Continuum book, we discovered something rather comical.

In sharing the working subtitle — "A How-To Guide for Shitty Leaders to Become Less Shitty Through Active Leadership" — a strange pattern emerged. The hundreds of people we spoke with said the same thing when reading the tagline: "I need a copy of that book for my current boss" or "my previous bosses!" Not a single person declared, "Maybe I should get a copy for myself."

Through this unregulated mini-survey, hundreds of individuals were quick to confirm their belief that shitty leadership existed — but that it was something they received, something they'd experienced, and never inflicted on anyone else. Everyone was eager to cite their experiences under shitty leadership but neglected to share moments when they may have been that shitty leader — what shitty leadership behaviours they may have demonstrated. Is that a coincidence? That's the by-product of a lack of awareness.

Are you self-aware enough to know you're self-aware?

People can quickly and easily recognise what shitty leadership means; "Oh, yeah, I know a shitty leader. Yeah, I work for three of them!" Everyone knows one, but no one wants to admit they are one, which exacerbates the epidemic. It creates a disengaged workforce, which most places don't even recognise they have — they don't realise that is exactly what has been impeding their profits. That is what is killing their return on investment. That is making them need more customers, clients and employees.

But why can't people seem to recognise shitty leadership in themselves? Is it because they don't understand how shitty leadership is defined? Could it be that they initially assumed that shitty leadership means shitty people? Who wants to openly admit that?

But shitty leadership does not mean shitty people. Shitty leadership is made up of behaviours. When people tell us, they know plenty of shitty leaders, I just ask them: "So you were on the receiving end of that shitty leadership. How did that feel?"

Take a behaviour that you're on the receiving end of and link it to a feeling or an action, that humanises it.

My boss yells at me because he's a shitty leader, and I feel shame. I feel blamed. I feel he treats me like a child. I have what I call 'Sunday despair'; feeling down before returning to a shitty job with a shitty boss on Monday. I don't want to go to work. I hate my job.

When you're on the receiving end of shitty leadership behaviours a majority of the time, it can take its toll in many ways, and the results are usually not positive.

Well, after they'd explained that, attached it to behaviour, and humanised that behaviour, I'd turn it around and ask, "So how many times have you caused that for others?"

That is the concept behind this global epidemic. It's the fact that some people don't want to talk about it. People don't understand it. Yet everyone can identify his or her own shitty leadership demonstrating bosses; everyone is so quick to pass judgement, but no one is willing to hold that mirror up and say, "Wow — I could really use some help with this too."

At this point, about 10–15% of the people we spoke turned around and started taking it out on the person asking the question — usually me. They got defensive, angry, or refused to talk. But don't shoot the messenger! If you find yourself getting defensive at this point, that's normal. Just don't let it be the end, and know that we can take it. Be self-aware!

Everyone has the ability to demonstrate better leadership. What it really boils down to is a willingness to embrace that change. If you are open to change and growth, and seek it out, you will find it.

If you put your employees first, the customer will follow. Your employees don't work for you: you're there to support them. It's about who you are as a person, and how you want to be defined as a leader. Leadership has so many layers to it, as we discussed when our journey began in Book One. We now have the opportunity to carry it even further.

INNOVATIVE DISRUPTION

Book One was our introduction. It was our initial mantra. This book will provide more insight into working through the discomfort felt by many people when they realise *they* were the shitty leader! We hope to support you with this.

Innovative disruption is about facing that discomfort, that aversion to change, and turning to embrace it. It's okay to feel uncomfortable. But you're not alone. The best changes occur when you put in the most work.

Self-awareness feels like a dangerous word. It's been in mainstream media for many years. Still, people don't really understand what it means. How do we know we're self-aware? How do we realise we're demonstrating shitty leadership behaviours? Because we don't see the world as it is; we see the world as we are. Everyone's got a different lens. One of the keys to becoming more self-aware is being able to look through your eyes with someone else's lens. It's a little bit like empathy.

Some readers will turn away at this point, thinking, "What does empathy have to do with my job?" What does all this touchy-feely stuff have to do with our bottom line?

I get it. You're tough. You don't want to show feelings at work. But what if 'showing your feelings' means you get that 41% reduction in absenteeism? What if I told you that if you changed 10% of your hard-nosed, shitty leadership behaviours, you could gain 21% in profitability? What if I told you that, over six months, you could save millions of pounds or dollars by changing your behaviour?

Does it all seem touchy-feely now?

I didn't think so. Think about how you treat your children. Think about how you treat your mother. That's vulnerability — when you're kind. Why is it so hard to act the same way in the workplace? Aside from the fact that every human being you encounter deserves to be treated with kindness — we can talk about that another time. Right now, what I'd like to focus on is how to help your business improve. Because if you're a shitty leader, I guarantee you've got a lot of rework issues. If you want to be a little bit kinder and more vulnerable and lead people in the way they prefer to be led, you will change your company culture — you can change your bottom line.

If you're ready to give it a try, treat this as your first test of vulnerability. If reading this feels difficult, if this feels really uncomfortable, own it. Go with it, because it's okay. I guarantee you, as soon as you rip that plaster off and start to deal with it, you will begin to feel better, or at least start to think about this more.

This is how you make your comfort zone bigger. People talk about stepping out of their comfort zone. But that's not always the answer. Make your comfort zone *bigger*.

Expand your own limits, don't step outside of it. That's what innovative disruption is all about.

Choosing to make your comfort zone bigger is key as it's your choice; you own the growth. Not simply stepping outside of it, which can feel accidental and temporary. You're growing and proving to yourself that you're choosing not to let your fear halt your growth.

For example, I absolutely loathe spiders. If I found one in my house, I would either have to leave temporarily until it was found, or move home if not. I hosted a work retreat a couple of years ago where I led a change exercise. We brought in a third-party company and bent arrows and metal bars with our necks, broke wooden boards with our hands and walked on fire. It was incredibly inspirational. When we shared fears, I told the group of 60 my fear of spiders. On the second day of the retreat, they bought me a gift. I opened the small box and inside was a big, fat hairy (fake) spider. I saw it, retrieved it and kissed it. In the past, I would have screamed and ran. My newfound confidence was a big deal for me.

To this day, I no longer have to move home when a spider comes to visit, and I attempt to lead it outside wherever possible. I've chosen not to let my fears continue. That's not a temporary decision. My comfort zone expanded because I chose to believe I could do it.

Innovative disruption means making innovations inside yourself. Disrupt what you're doing out of habit or ignorance, and try to be innovative in your approach to change. The more you buy into this innovation, the more you'll be able to recognise that things are going to feel weird. This is going to feel uncomfortable. This is disruptive, provocative stuff that will turn you into a self-aware leader able to give their people what they need.

It's a disruption because it's not the way things are working right now. Imagine if 80% of a company's leaders decided to buy into this. What would happen to that workforce? Very, very quickly, people would start to enjoy coming to work. People would begin to feel supported, instead of shamed. People would start to feel aligned and informed instead of ignored. When you have an engaged and aligned workforce, you will be shocked at how much productivity soars, and how much your cost of rework diminishes.

When that starts happening in the organisation, several different things start as a by-product. You will start to see less sick time. You will start to see less clock watching. And who do you think is going to *really* notice this? Customers. Remember, your customer does *not* come first. Your employees do. Because if you treat your employees well, the customer will follow. If you forget about your employees, your customers will forget about you. It's really that simple.

YOUR LEADERSHIP BRAND AND YOUR PERFORMANCE

What exactly is a 'leadership brand'? A leadership brand is one of the components of active leadership. The first step in beginning the self-awareness process is to know yourself and how you lead. How do you want to be branded as a leader? How are you currently perceived as a leader? Do you know the difference?

There are two components to this: how you see yourself — and how others see you. First, allow yourself to explore how you really feel in these areas. Then, ask those you feel safe with to engage in that dialogue with you. If you want to challenge yourself to continue to expand your comfort zone, ask for feedback from someone you don't mesh well with. See if extending an olive branch alters the current relationship.

There are three main components to review when you're trying to identify what your leadership brand is. The first question to ask yourself is related to your leadership style:

› Who are you as a leader, and what does that mean?
› Are you data-driven?
› Are you people focused?
› Are you linear?
› Are you creative?

Really search to find out who you are as a leader. One way to do this is to ask yourself: what do people get when they work for you or with you?

Then think about what's important to you:

› What are your values?
› Where do those values come from?
› How do you want to be perceived as a leader?
› Does that link in with your values and who you are?

Next, ask yourself what you need:

› What motivates you as a leader?
› Is it a passive workforce?
› Is it people who challenge you?
› Does knowing your staff's jobs motivate you?
› How do you feel if you don't know their jobs?
› Do you feel like you can still lead a team if you don't know what their roles are?
› How do you close those gaps?
› Then, what are your emotional triggers?
› What will trigger you emotionally within your role that may cause others to misperceive you?

When you put all that together, what you're talking about is starting to identify who you are as a leader, and how you want to be perceived as one. It means developing your brand and then owning it. I have my own leadership brand: I am a creative person. I'm not naturally linear, but I can be when I have to be. When I work with someone who is very linear and data-driven, I let them know that I'm more on the creative side, but I'm happy to be flexible. In many instances, they will probably be more linear than I am, and I am comfortable owning it.

I'm all about *people, people, people, people*. I am a highly intuitive, creative thinker. If I ask a question, it's not because I'm trying to test you. It's because I don't know the answer, and I want to know. I will take feedback delivery as a very important piece of our relationship. I will find out how you prefer to receive feedback, and then I will deliver it to you in that way. If I fail to do this, I ask that you stop me and remind me, so that I deliver it in the way that's best for you. I expect you to manage up and challenge me. If I don't get it right, I'm okay with that.

I will lead by democracy wherever possible. If I have to be a dictator, I will be, and I will tell you why. I wear my emotions on my sleeve. It doesn't mean I respond to events emotionally, but rather that I am willing to show my emotions. I am comfortable showing how I am feeling but I am in control of it. I am choosing to show my emotions rather than respond emotively. I am all for simplicity and not overcomplicating anything. I really do like things to be kept simple and for some fun to be had while we're at work.

This is my leadership brand.

This is what people get when they work for or with me. Now, imagine you were on my team, and it was our first day working together, and I shared all of that with you. I can build trust more quickly because I can prove to you that I am who I say I am — because *I've declared who I am*. That is a leadership brand. Show your staff who you are. Tell them who you are. Then hold yourself accountable to that. If you haven't connected this yet, get ready. This is also a display of vulnerability. Not a weakness, but a strength. Leaders aren't perfect or smarter than their staff. That is old school thinking that contributes to shitty behaviours and perceptions. It's completely acceptable to show your staff you're also human. Keep reading.

This is key for performance development as it builds trust. When you have trust in your relationship, you *will* get more out of your employees. It creates an open door, comfortable scenario that gives people what they need to actually lead their performance in the right way. Managing performance eventually becomes irrelevant, because you're setting the tone for them to manage their own performance. That's what makes a great leader. It also fosters simplicity as a core value within your organisation. How does that value reduce error and rework?

When your employees trust you, and you're setting them up to succeed, and they're feeling engaged and safe, that leads them to perform at a higher level. It starts to create alignment. They feel like their leader has their back. They feel like they have a leader. It makes them want to do things differently. It reduces the quit-and-stay. It reduces the apathy. It motivates and inspires.

During one consulting gig years ago, we interviewed contact centre advisors to explore why their process quality scores were so weak. We discussed the plan going forward in small groups of three to five advisors, and how changes would help them improve, should they choose to embrace them. When we told the advisors that their team managers would support them, one said, "I have a team manager?" I replied, "Oh, my apologies, I didn't realise you were so new, let's find out who your lead is." She said, "I've worked here eight months!" Some organisations just don't get it. Eight months on the job, poor quality scores, no feedback and they hire a consultant to fix it? Talk about an expensive rework initiative! Do you see the connections?

If these insights are new for you, it's going to feel uncomfortable. It's going to feel challenging. Find the inner courage to keep going, because the light at the end of the tunnel is so much brighter. Then you go into your leadership brand, which talks about who are you as a leader and how you want to be defined. Let your staff know that if you deviate from this, they should feel comfortable holding you accountable. If you talk about who you are as a leader and you own it, you're teaching your staff to manage up when you fall off your frequency road. This is essential to build trust, reduce disengagement and create more effective leadership perceptions. Then, you ask those two questions from Book One:

> How do you like to be led?
> How do you like to receive feedback?

These questions not only equip you, but they also build trust, empathy and humility. Then, when you have to provide constructive feedback, you're able to deliver it and it actually makes a difference.

That's how we get from A to B.

This book is going to break down all of those sections on a much deeper level.

HOW THIS AFFECTS TRAINING

If you look at training from a performance perspective, most companies that suffer from shitty leadership environments or toxic cultures tend to miss the boat on training. Because, and I hate to burst your bubble on this, generalised training models don't work. Adult learning model techniques and how adults learn should be based on the demographic of your employee population — baby boomers and millennials don't learn in the same way. They have different core values and see things differently, so of course, they learn differently!

Don't think of it as training. Think of it as learning. Figure out *what they already know*, and then teach them the rest. Then, what you're actually doing is linking everything together.

Here's an example to explain what I mean: I was hired by a company to come in and start an end-to-end journey of the employee experience. The first thing I did was change how employees were recruited. Instead of a standard interview process, we started holding auditions. We had open calls and did group drama games, which allowed the recruits to play interactively as a team and demonstrate certain competencies. We didn't ask them what they could do; we got them to show us. We did it in a way that was focused on adult learning — we were hiring contact centre advisors, not actors.

This process reduced recruitment time by 75% and saved $75 to $200 per head, per recruitment, per candidate hired. Plus, right off the bat, that employee's experience was completely different. We reduced induction time. We made it about learning instead of training. We figured out what they already knew, and taught the rest. We made it interactive and experiential.

Then, they graduated from the academy and began working on the contact centre floor. They had team managers and team leaders who were non-shitty in their leadership, who were all about them and not about themselves, and it was the best induction class the company had seen in years. Their results were stellar. And guess what?

There was zero attrition.

It was the *first* time a new hire inductee class had 0% attrition. Everyone stayed. Why? Because they were valued. They were aligned. They were happy. They were informed. They felt set up for success. Why the hell would they go anywhere else?

ABOUT MARK

I am a leadership consultant, business coach, speaker, and author of the first book in this series: *The Ego Continuum* (here on out referred to as Book One). I am a reformed shitty leader and a certified professional coach, and I have personally led and coached thousands of individuals, working with top companies in Canada, the U.S. and the UK. Having worked with many shitty leaders, I've become pretty good at helping those ready to figure out how to remove the blame/shame game and actually make changes in their leadership.

My experience writing Book One evoked every possible human emotion repeatedly, and to extremes. I'm sitting here thinking about it, and it's completely overwhelming, in a good way. I remember my own struggles with authority and reflect on my own shitty leadership moments. Then I think about when we launched Book One: within five days, we went from 44 Facebook likes on our company page to over

20,000. That tells me that people really want, and need, to read this, I say humbly!

That feedback sparked me to keep going and take this to a deeper level. If you're ready to hold up a mirror, you deserve someone showing you how. Because that's the first part of getting rid of shitty leadership behaviour: forcing yourself to look in the mirror, honestly and authentically, and being okay with the fact that you might not like what you see.

> **It's time to make some changes.**

If you're ready, keep reading.

READY FOR SOME SELF-ASSESSMENT?

So now what? You recognise that things have to change. You recognise that it is your fear of change that's stopping you, so you're going to try to choose to be vulnerable. You know that you're not always the best leader you can be, but you're going to continue to move forward and do your best to change.

How do you move forward? Well, we've got the first step right here. It takes some bravery to do this — but here's the good news: it's all inside your head. This isn't public. No one's going to know the answers to these questions but you. Are you ready to look in the mirror?

SELF-ASSESSMENT QUESTIONS:

Are you ready and open to change? How do you know you're ready? Reflect on a time when you were on the receiving end of constructive feedback.

› Who was it from?

> Was it solicited or unsolicited?
> Was it feedback or opinion?
> What was the intention?
> How did you respond?

Think about the last time you gave feedback because you wanted to 'teach' the person a lesson. Did you want to be right?

Does reflecting on these areas help you to accept that maybe there is some validity in taking a look at this in more detail? What do you have to lose? What about on a personal level? We talk a lot about shitty leader/employee relationships, but what about outside of work?

A SUMMARY OF THE INTRODUCTION

You have to lead yourself. You have to be self-aware and actually make choices, actually decide what direction you want to be going. Everything we do in life is a choice. Then when you apply it, when you're trying to lead others, you're really making it about relationships. This is absolutely going to be uncomfortable for many of you — but research tells us it is the best choice you can make for your business. After you develop a leadership brand and master the ability to effectively deliver feedback in a way that is specific to each individual, that leads to active leadership, which then drives performance.

Our first book set the stage and revealed the problem; this book will show you what to do when you realise *you're* part of the problem!

ONE

What Does Being a Shitty Leader Really Mean

> My name is Mark Robinson, and I declare myself a reformed shitty leader.

My passion comes from helping people, which was developed through my own experiences and the support I've received throughout my career and personal life. I developed the Ego Continuum methodology over a period of many years, working with some amazing people. Some of these people, myself included, were shitty leaders. They demonstrated behaviours that were unproductive in the workplace and in the development of their staff, or, rather, the lack of development of their staff. They were on the receiving end of unproductive behaviours. The receiving end of unproductive behaviours is subjective, and everyone will react differently to a variety of situations — this is normal human behaviour. With more than seven billion people inhabiting the planet, there are bound to be different reactions to the same behaviours.

Like some of you, I have also been on the receiving end of poorly delivered feedback and bullying, both at school and in the workplace. My personal journey is not unique, or much different to many others, but we all have a story. I'm just choosing to tell mine here.

I was morbidly obese for over 20 years. I never thought things would change. I tried hundreds, if not thousands, of tips and tricks and programs, and would do just about anything to try and shed pounds. I felt isolated. I felt shunned. I felt ridiculed. My self-worth was low. I did not believe I was worthy of love or a meaningful connection, so my interactions with others were skewed. They were based on how I thought I should be for them, versus who I really was, and what I was able to bring to the table. That impacted on all of my connections: personal, family, and work-related. I had trouble maintaining long-term relationships, and I wasn't able to communicate clearly.

Somehow, through my own wickedly sharp ability to laugh at most things, my survival stemmed from a belief that change was always inevitable. Even though I was morbidly obese and unhappy, upset with myself, hiding behind a wall — I could still laugh. My motto and life mission was, "*This too shall pass.*"

We all have a story, and we have the ability to share the parts we are comfortable sharing. Some more than others. The Ego Continuum framework and methodology were born from my experiences, from a place of hope, passion, and the desire that, together, we might actually create a better place to work, and more, simply by knowing who we are and how we treat others.

I've experienced thinking, "*I didn't do this as well as I could have,*" as well as "*I haven't been treated as well as I could have,*" and I accept that behaviours can change. People are not defined and shouldn't be defined by their last behaviour. Right?

But they do have to find change or the cycle will continue. Shitty leadership breeds more shitty leadership. They can hold the mirror up, but they have to actually open their eyes, and see through an authentic lens. And by "they", of course, I mean you. Because you're the one reading this book, aren't you?

So, let's hold up a mirror.

WHAT EXACTLY IS A SHITTY LEADER?

A common shitty leadership behaviour is making most events or situations about them. They are skewed with an internal lens that influences behaviours. Many don't realise they are demonstrating these behaviours, which contributes to the global epidemic. A shitty leader doesn't focus on active leadership and is, in fact, an *in*active leader. A shitty leader negatively impacts corporate culture and doesn't realise that they are contributing to a disengaged workforce.

They might think they're actively leading, mostly because they're either bullying or micromanaging. Two very different extremes. If you're an inactive leader, your lens is skewed: many of your behavioural outputs will most likely be counterproductive.

Shitty leaders don't proactively recognise their staff. They don't consider their own or staffs' behaviour. They yell, they blame, they shame. They are not aware of the shadows they cast. They create toxicity.

They are not people-focused. They are not company-focused. They are focused on themselves. They may appear focused to some, as they drive results, but they leave behind a trail of misery. Is that a productive and engaged corporate culture?

Of course, we can recognise these leaders easily — we all have stories. Except for when we look at ourselves in the mirror. But before we get ahead of ourselves, there's one thing we all need to agree on, and that's what shitty leadership is *not*.

WHAT A SHITTY LEADER ISN'T

A shitty leader is not a shitty person. Let me repeat: a shitty leader is not (necessarily) a shitty person. I'm not here to tell you that you're a terrible person. It's quite possible — and even common — for good people to demonstrate shitty leadership behaviours. Shitty leadership is not about your personality; it's about your behaviour. Personality is who you are. Behaviour is what you do.

Often, people hear me speak or coach and they become resistant because they think I'm suggesting they change their personality. That's not what this is about at all. Your personality is valuable. It's you. It's inherently beautiful (in my opinion). Your behaviour might not match up with that. Your behaviour might simply be counterproductive in the workplace, at times!

I'm not interested in changing who people are. I'm interested in changing what people do. I'm not trying to transform people into clones or robots. What I'm trying to help you recognise is how you can stay in control of your behaviours, so that you can be a more productive leader and give your staff what *they* need to be effective, drive results in your workplace and establish an engaged workforce.

THE POSSIBILITIES OF NON-SHITTY LEADERSHIP

An employee once sent me an email stating that he didn't like my tone. Clearly, it was his perception of my tone, as we were talking about an email. There was a misunderstanding and some confusion on both parts. I chose not to respond via email, but to pick up the phone and have a chat. I opted for kindness and understanding, as a way of trying to determine what had happened and how he had come to his perception.

That's a non-shitty leadership approach. Other people might have said "I don't give a shit if you don't like my tone. You are my employee. Do as you're told. Don't ever send me an email like that again. Are we clear?"

But then, what would that have done? If he already had an issue reporting to me, which I suspect he did, I would have made that worse. I would have been making it about me, not about him.

How did I discern what he needed? Because I'm an active leader, and I'd taken the time to get to know him and understand what he was all about. Our original interaction was not based on anything to do with me. I know that because I know what he was going through on a personal level.

Knowing your team is essential as what they need today might not be what they need tomorrow. That's why it's called *active* leadership.

The two questions from the first book must be revisited continuously: how do they like to be led? And how do they like to receive feedback? Keep asking those questions. Spot check regularly, to see if anything has changed. If someone is going through a difficult period in his or her personal life, they might never show it, or they might show it all the time!

If things look or feel different, check to make sure you're still leading in the way that they need. Someone could be really strong, courageous and independent (the type of person who likes clear and direct feedback) but if they're going through a bad break-up or divorce, they might now need a softer approach. As active leaders, it's up to us to figure that out.

Don't get me wrong here: we don't have to go into grave details about personal life. We don't have to play psychiatrist — that's a slippery slope. Just make it your job to be aware of who your folks are. If their behaviours are changing because of outside influences, you should pick up on this, because you are actively leading.

RECAP

Shitty leadership is inactive leadership. We all know leaders like that — but it's hard to recognise that behaviour in ourselves. Part of the problem is that we equate shitty leaders with shitty people, which couldn't be further from the truth. Good people can be shitty leaders. Shitty leadership is not about your personality, and we don't want to try and change your personality. Shitty leadership is about your behaviour, and when you choose to change your behaviours to non-shitty ones, you will make powerful, long-term differences within your team. It all begins with choosing *active* leadership.

TWO

Shitty Leader Behaviours

Think about a shitty leader you have worked with, or for. What behaviours did they demonstrate that led you to identify them as shitty? Next, think about when you worked with them. How did it feel to be on the receiving end? Finally, think about when you demonstrated the same behaviours. Could you have incited others to feel the same way you did?

CLASSIC BEHAVIOURS OF A SHITTY LEADER

What are the common behaviours of shitty leaders? What does a shitty boss do? What does a shitty leader do or say that creates those common outcomes? First of all, they play the blame and shame game. They're all about shifting blame to anyone but themselves. They're tactless, they have no decorum, or they're rude — whether it's the pressures of leadership, their own insecurities or something else, they've let go of social niceties in the worst way. They micromanage, they don't ask, they knock people down. They are perceived as unapproachable or toxic. They are unaware of the shadows they cast on their team. They are inconsistent with their actions, they have unclear objectives, and they cause confusion. They might demand that you create a certain PowerPoint, which you work frantically to complete, only to insist this wasn't what they asked for.

They use harsh tones (they might even be verbally abusive), and they almost certainly lack listening skills. They hear, but they don't listen. They're on their phone when they should be listening in a meeting, or talking. They are perceived as being outside their leadership brand, or not even having one. Or they just don't seem to care. They're usually always very busy and have no issues ensuring everyone knows this. Of course, shitty leaders don't necessarily demonstrate all of these behaviours all the time. There are no limits here. Sometimes these demonstrated behaviours are the perceptions of others, and not necessarily reality. However, whether you're perceived as a shitty leader or truly are a shitty leader, the outcomes are the same.

Such workplaces have low morale, high turnover, and soul-sapping, numbing toxicity that leads to burnout.

Everything that you can think of that makes a workplace purgatory — if not hell — is because of this poor leadership and the associated outcomes. The list of behaviours and actions are not mutually exclusive. They are vast and subjective.

WORKPLACE RESULTS OF CLASSIC SHITTY LEADERSHIP

When you're on the receiving end of shitty leadership, you feel isolated, and you give up; it feels like Sunday despair, which I touched upon earlier.

You might be thinking "*Oh, not again!*" or "*How does he or she constantly get away with this? I'll show them, I quit!*", or "*I can't take it anymore, I'm done, forget this place, I just don't want to be here.*"

Or you might be silent — because you've stopped caring. You will quit and leave — or you will quit and stay. This enforces apathy and breeds harsh venting, where people become victims. It creates an 'us and them' culture. It erodes trust, increases unnatural attrition and impacts on clients and customers in negative ways. It feels awful; like constant negativity.

When you're constantly feeling down, you're choosing to be in a low frequency — and when you're constantly in a low frequency, it can be really hard to pick yourself up and see the forest through the trees.

SHITTY LEADERSHIP IN ACTION

"If you're thinking of coming over to talk to me now, think again," she said, in front of others. I immediately did an about-face, as who wants to be spoken to in that way? She was really busy, very stressed and working to tight a deadline, so of course, that was a completely acceptable way to speak to a peer. (That was sarcasm, in case you missed the intended humour!)

Sometimes, shitty leadership behaviours last only a short moment. They are not usual behaviours, but emotional outbursts as a result of individuals not allowing themselves to remain in control. We all have deadlines at times. We're all busy. It's never an excuse to be disrespectful and rude. If she had been more self-aware, she would have paused and taken accountability for her tone and words, and simply indicate when she would be free to talk.

There is always room for kindness. We're all human, and it happens, but we also need to be accountable for our actions. Or is that being an adult? I mix those two up sometimes. (Yup, sarcasm again!)

RECAP

Overall, we can recognise this: there are classic shitty leadership behaviours that incite strong feelings for those on the receiving end. The negativity can have ramifications in the workplace for individuals and for the team. Some of these behaviours resurface regularly, time and time again, like bullying or blaming, and that can help us recognise shitty leadership.

Now, at this point in our journey, you have identified what a shitty leader is — you can recognise it. You might even be open to the idea of saying "Okay, *I* might do those things sometimes...I'm not sure yet." These behaviours might belong to you, but you're still figuring them out. You are, hopefully, understanding what shitty leadership behaviour really means.

Remember, it *doesn't* mean you're a shitty person. It just means you might need to take control in a positive manner.

Change is needed, for everyone's sake.

More importantly: you are part of the change.

You can also control how you react and internalise it all, too. More to come on that soon.

THREE

Connecting Behaviours to Actions & Feelings

Everyone has power over his or her own feelings — no one can 'make' a person feel a certain way. However, shitty leaders can push buttons; shitty leaders can incite feelings in others, making it hard for those on the receiving end to react positively. You've felt that; a shitty leader has no doubt incited you. You can choose your emotions, but their behaviours make it difficult to choose wisely. However, who is ultimately accountable for YOU?

Understanding what a shitty leader is and how a shitty leader behaves means you now understand that you might be working for a shitty leader and suffering the negative impacts of that. Now it's time to look in the mirror and ask questions of you.

This is about how you've incited negative reactions in other people. How you've pushed their buttons and made their choices extremely difficult. It can be hard to digest that we have incited others to feel things like isolation, anger, Sunday despair, anxiety, etc. The good news? You have the power of choice.

HAVE I DONE THIS TO OTHERS?

How many times have you made others feel this way?

A team manager attended an Ego Continuum leadership workshop and then read our first book. He provided some fantastic feedback. As he was reading and reflecting, he realised certain areas of his own leadership style. He recognised that he wasn't always as approachable as he should be and that he could spend more time understanding how best to deliver feedback to each receiver as an individual. He bought into the concept of non-cookie cutter leadership quite well and embraced these concepts quickly.

He began by reframing his one-on-one sessions with his team, and in a few short weeks, the team had new life. Many provided great feedback and were so impressed with his level of attention and support. The impacts of his chosen behaviours inspired others to do more. One of his staff said, "This feels like a new place to work!" The power of effective leadership is stronger than you think. Are you thinking more?

If you've ever said, "Nothing ever changes here!" you're mistaken. It's not the workplace that has to change — it's you.

Once you learn this stuff, you can't unlearn it. Non-shitty leadership can seep into every area of your life — in a wonderful way. With your family, your partner, your children, your friends — it's not just for corporate culture.

The concepts of right versus kind, the power of choice, seeking to understand another person's point of view and diffusing situations through effective communication? All of those make for success in all areas of your life.

By learning non-shitty behaviours, you are unlearning the shitty behaviours.

THE EMOTIONAL CONSEQUENCES OF THE EPIPHANY

Right now, you may be having an epiphany. You're realising that you have, in fact, demonstrated shitty leadership behaviours. Or perhaps you realised this earlier in the book.

Not too long ago, I was facilitating a corporate workshop on the Ego Continuum. We went over the introduction, covering *what is* a shitty leader. In the group of about 20 people, I had folks from three levels of leadership: from Senior Contact Centre Managers, to Team Managers, to Team Supervisors. They all worked together at this one company, and although they knew the workshop was coming, I deliberately didn't go into a lot of detail. They were looking forward to it, but were probably a little apprehensive about this workshop.

I started by asking them all: "Who has worked for a shitty leader in the past?" Of course, everyone put their hand up. Everyone said that they had previously worked for a shitty leader. They all knew behaviours they could discuss right away. I broke them up into teams, and they started writing those behaviours down.

Then we talked about actions and feelings — and we linked how it felt to be on the receiving end. Everyone was engaged; they were laughing, they were listening. There was a little bit of lecturing, but it was mainly group work. Everyone was enjoying themselves.

And then I asked the question: "So how many of you have caused, or incited, others to feel this way?"

The room went silent. How did *that* feel? That's when we started talking about shame.

I remember one person said: "It feels really awkward right now, because I am reflecting in ways that I've never reflected before, and I realise all the times that I have made people feel this way."

I told her, "It was so brave of you to be vulnerable and share that. That was fantastic. What you're feeling right now is our version of change, and it's called Innovative Disruption. This feels disruptive. This feels provocative. It's controversial, and it's okay. Don't beat yourself up. Don't give in to self-shame and lower your self-worth because you're recognising that, at times, you've treated people this way. That won't be productive."

As the day continued, the mood never really changed. People were making notes. People were really listening. It was fascinating to be on the receiving end of that because they were starting to get it, and I could see the epiphany moments. I could sense the reflections in the room. I could feel people reflecting in front of me.

As you're having this epiphany, you might be feeling shame, too. You might be hanging your head like they were. But what I said to that employee on that day applies to you, too: It's okay. This feels hard; it feels upsetting. Let that be okay. Just don't beat yourself up about it. You are not defined by your past behaviour; you've recognised the need for change, and you are capable of that change. Don't let this shame lower your self-worth; remind yourself that you are capable of better, and this feeling will pass.

Embrace the disruption.

EMBRACING INNOVATIVE DISRUPTION

Sometimes the change you make can seem minor — but it makes an amazing difference in the long run. One of the men at the same workshop told me how, in his team, there was a lot of confusion about some of the employee rules; the corporate stuff. So, when the new handbook came out, he shared it with everyone and highlighted some of the points that they were requesting. Then he said, "If you have any questions, let me know."

This might not seem like a lot. The thing is, in the past, no one ever did that kind of thing. They didn't address confusion; the old him, the shitty leader, would have just tossed the handbook at them and left them to figure it out alone. There was just no communication. See, minor differences can have massive impacts, in a positive way.

This time, however, he intentionally challenged himself: "What can I do differently?" The smallest effort made a maximum change. The whole team was more unified, more confident, more efficient — because he'd given them what they needed in a supportive way that removed the confusion. That's alignment.

The other thing is, when he was telling me this story, I saw a new confidence in him. I saw a new light in his eyes. He was a new person. He knew he could change, he knew he could be a better leader — and he was ready to embrace it.

Now, if you're reading this book, and you're painfully aware that you won't be receiving feedback — that your new leadership will have to be implemented by you, and you alone — there are plenty of ways to track your improvement. Try counting how many times you hear your staff members or teammates say, "You've never asked me that before," or "No one's ever asked me that before."

Think about the times where you can see that you've created a reflective moment for someone else. Pay attention to their behaviour; the leader in that story saw his team happy and engaged, and that's not normal behaviour. He saw the fruits of his own labour.

That's another epiphany moment: "*Oh, wow*", you'll say to yourself, "*this really works!*"

The reverse can work, too. If you're having trouble figuring out whether or not you really are a shitty leader, watch your employees' behaviour. Check how your team behaves. If there's disengaged or demoralised behaviour going on, there's a problem. And, as the leader, it almost always stems from you. Even if you do nothing, that's doing something.

Silence is consent.

YOUR POWER OF CHOICE

In Book One, we talked a lot about how Eleanor Roosevelt said, "No one makes you feel inferior without your consent." It is one of my favourite quotes of all time — that's what the power of choice is all about.

If you and I are having a discussion, and you say to me, "Mark, you just hurt my feelings. I'm angry", I think about what happened. My words travelled across the airwaves and went into your ear, at which point you assimilated the information and determined how you were going to react to it — all within a mega millisecond.

But here's the thing: did my words actually hurt you, or did you choose to be hurt?

If I said to you, "I think you're absolutely lovely," you probably wouldn't be offended by that — you wouldn't choose to be offended. But what if I said, "You know what? I think you're an idiot", you might choose to be offended. And yes, it is a choice, because everything that we say to each other goes through our own filters of: why are you telling me this? Why do I need to know this? Why should I care?

If I call you an idiot, you don't have to get mad. You could say, "Why are you saying that?" When you apply that lens to any communication, you always have a choice.

Now, if someone were to call me an idiot, I am authentic and self-aware enough to know that sometimes, I can demonstrate idiotic behaviour. If someone is telling me I am behaving like one, and they mean it, odds are I probably am. Because I can be an idiot sometimes. So, I say thank you for the feedback! If someone I don't know calls me an idiot, and I don't care about their opinion, it's probably going to be water off a duck's back.

Now, I can be sensitive at times, depending upon the interaction. When I get angry emails, I have a 20-second guttural thought process of *"Who the hell do you think you are?!"*

But, that's just my initial state. I recognise it instantly and return to being calm. I find my frequency. I no longer make it about me; I make it about them, thinking, *"She doesn't normally send me emails like that. It must be because of this; it must be because of that."* I take a deep breath, and I respond from a place of kindness.

This choice is what we call not taking the bait. It's about retaining your non-shitty leadership brand by responding from a place of kindness.

Now, I want to be very clear: this doesn't mean that you can never react to anything. If your team member or employee frustrates you, it's okay to tell them that. As long as you're still kind. Whenever you're in an argument with someone, especially someone you work with, remember that you're on the same team. You don't need to get defensive and make sure you win, that you're right. You need to be kind. It doesn't have to be an emotive response.

You can still say, "Look, this is really bothering me. This is what I want to talk about." You can show your honest emotions without it being a blame game, as long as you remember that the other person is still on your team — and you're supposed to be on theirs.

THE POWER OF CHOICE IN ACTION

In the customer service industry world, I make a very bold statement. I say: there isn't an escalation I can't diffuse.

Most contact centres have a three-strikes policy. If a customer is using profanity, the contact centre will teach their staff in induction to say, "Sir, madam, if you continue to use that vulgar language, I will have no choice but to terminate this call." When you talk to a customer that's already irate, is that going to diffuse the situation?

When I go in as a consultant, the first thing I recommend for call centres is to get rid of that three-strikes rule. Instead, replace it with empathy statements. Authentic, genuine, power of choice empathy statements. Because here's the truth: most human beings don't call you for the sole purpose of dropping f-bombs. How did they get to that angry place?

How much time have they wasted in order to get to this call? How much incompetence in our company have they faced?

So, when they're angry, you listen. You say, "Sir, madam, I can hear by your words and the tone of your voice that you're very upset by the situation. I realise that this was probably caused by something we did or didn't do. I want you to know that you've reached the right person. I'm going to take complete ownership of this situation. We will get this resolved today so that we don't waste any more of your time. How does that sound?"

But that's not what most employees will do. Most employees will say to themselves, "*I'm not paid to deal with this nonsense!*" and get out as soon as they can.

Now, why do employees do that? Could it be that they are disengaged because they work for a shitty leader? A leader who doesn't give them feedback, who doesn't have their back, who doesn't give them room to grow?

This all comes back to the power of choice — but here, you, as the leader, have to show your team what their choices are, and how to choose their responses productively. The power of choice for leaders trickles down to their employees every time. Remember the mountain from the first page? Remember, we don't see the world as it is; we see the world as we see ourselves.

When a leader takes responsibility to coach and give feedback to staff, people stop fearing those irate calls. They stop fearing their job. They change their lens, and when they face those stressful situations, they can ask and learn what incited such a reaction. They realise they don't have to respond with anger or put up a wall, they know their leader has their back.

CHOICE AND THE POSSIBILITIES FOR GREAT LEADERSHIP

I did a project years ago on executive escalations and was tasked with a 50% reduction. In one year, 77% of escalations were executive. We then looked at those escalations to try and discover the initial and secondary root causes — why the customer initially called, and why the call escalated. Guess what we discovered?

86% of the internal escalations that went executive were due to agent or advisor behaviour. The advisor who was supposed to resolve the customer issue the first time was the prime reason why the escalation escalated further. They were causing it themselves.

If those advisors changed their lens, if they unlearned that initial three-strikes tape and started to do things differently, started diffusing those calls, how would that affect them? Not just the customer — how would it affect the advisor? How would it make them feel? How would they feel about themselves? How would their confidence be affected? How would it change how they are perceived? How would it impact on their job satisfaction? What happens when they went home — how will they feel there? How will they now interact with their friends, families, partners, children? How will those people become better parents? When positive feelings emerge, people feel aligned and are positioned to make more positive choices.

This should be a win-win-win. It should be a win for the customers, a win for the employees, and a win for the leaders. And every time anybody is on the receiving or giving end of that win, that's a chance for them to take it somewhere else.

When you think about the links between identifying behaviours that are counterproductive in the workplace, that lead to a toxic culture and a disengaged workforce, and the behaviours that do the opposite, it's staggering. You realise that the powers leaders have are life changing. It's a cultural changer. It's a power that we have, that we shouldn't abuse.

Use your power for good.

BUT WHAT IF I'M NOT FEELING IT?

In theory, this is where you connect how you've felt on the receiving end of shitty leadership with those who face your shitty leadership. This is where you have empathy for those people. But what if you're not feeling it? How can you build empathy when you just don't feel it? Are you the type of person who just 'doesn't do feelings' at work?

This is where I believe the research of Dr Brené Brown is incredibly insightful. I refer to her TEDTalk from 2010 in Book One, and if you've not seen her lectures or read her books, I highly recommend you do. She shares in this TEDTalk how her research indicates that what separates people who experience a strong sense of love and belonging from those who struggle with this, is that those with a strong sense of love and belonging *believe they're worthy of it*. When studying the data collected from 'wholehearted' people, she discovered they had these things in common:

1. **Courage:** they were offering partners their whole hearts; they had the courage to be imperfect.
2. **Compassion:** these people were kind to themselves and to others.

3. **Connection:** their connections were rooted in authenticity; letting go of who they thought they should be to be who they were.
4. **Vulnerability:** they embraced vulnerability as something that was necessary for connection. Examples of vulnerability include asking someone for help, initiating intimacy with your partner when you could be rejected, waiting for the doctor to call back, getting laid off, laying people off.

Now, if you are living in that numb-land, if you 'don't do feelings' at work, there are negative repercussions to that, too. We cannot selectively numb our emotions. When we numb the negative feelings, we numb the positive ones, too. You can't avoid the qualities found in Dr Brown's research at work, but expect them to flourish in your personal life.

The people who say, "I don't do feelings" don't realise that this is a self-fulfilling prophecy. Because if you numb the things you are afraid of, like vulnerability, grief, shame, fear, and disappointment, then you're also numbing joy, gratitude, happiness and love.

In her research, Dr Brené Brown made the following statement about shame: "Shame can be understood as the fear of disconnection, the fear that there is something about me that makes others consider me unworthy of connection. Shame is universal. We all have it. The only people who don't experience shame have no capacity for human empathy or connection." There are people who claim they are not empathetic when truly they just have a fear of showing it.

Many don't want to talk about shame, but if you don't talk about it, you'll just get more of it. Shame is expressed in the feeling of "I am not 'blank' enough": good enough, thin enough, rich enough, beautiful enough, smart enough, promoted enough, etc. You might be feeling those things at some level. Where does that come from? How can you work through it?

If you're unsure how to develop your empathy, challenge yourself to do one thing differently with a member of your staff who is more on the vocal side. Ask them the two questions: how they like to be led, and how they like to receive feedback. Behave accordingly for two weeks and see what feedback they give you. Because let me tell you: when someone looks you in the face for the first time and says, "I can't tell you how much I appreciate the effort you have been making", you're going to end up feeling something.

You'll start to see empathy within yourself blooming, as you're connecting to your team. To other humans. People regularly report to me that they feel happier than ever before — because they feel like they're making a difference.

Welcome to human connection. Welcome to feeling worthy. We've been waiting for you to arrive.

If you practise putting yourself in other people's shoes, you quickly become aware of being more empathising. We're often rusty at that sort of thing because we're so focused on ourselves. As a leader, the practice of putting yourself in someone else's shoes makes empathy more and more accessible. We also call this lens awareness.

RECAP: THE POWER OF CHOICE & INNOVATIVE DISRUPTION

The Power of Choice:
The power of choice means we are responsible for our own behaviours; we choose how we respond. But that doesn't mean that we have no responsibility for our team. Yes, they can choose their own responses and emotions, but you have

the power to push their buttons, to cast a dark shadow. That's your responsibility, too.

We are accountable for how we choose to react. I had a negative conversation with someone a while back; she was just convinced that everything we were talking about was my fault. And I said, "Listen, you know what? This is how I'm feeling." I didn't say *you're* making me feel this way. But I did say, "Because of your behaviours, I am choosing to feel this. And I don't normally choose these feelings, so clearly, you've pushed my buttons, and I've let you. So how do we move forward from here?"

And she said to me, "Well, Mark, I'm not responsible for how you choose to feel." Yet her behaviours were inciting the way I was feeling, and it felt like she no longer had my back.

So, I said, "You know what? You are absolutely right," and I ended the connection. I pulled away as her lack of ownership became toxic. It over complicated something that should have been simple. Because she wanted to be right; and she's not responsible for my feelings. I am. I saw that she wasn't willing to negotiate; she was convinced that it was all me. I'm highly aware that we are the average of the five people we spend the most time with. So, I opted to move her out of that top five. By choice. It wasn't a question of me being right. It was a question of behaviour. If she didn't feel that she had done anything wrong, then there was an empathetic disconnection there. My choice is that I choose not to be around that type of behaviour.

I was able to say, "Our relationship feels negative and toxic. You're right; you're not accountable for my feelings, so I'm just going to move forward and wish you well. Some may choose to see that behaviour as emotive or childish, like deleting a friend on social media. When we take ownership

CONNECTING BEHAVIOURS TO ACTIONS & FEELINGS

of the toxic triggers in our life and remove them from the equation, is that being emotional or responsible? You decide!

Innovative Disruption:
You might be feeling shame. Is there shame in admitting you may demonstrate some of these behaviours? Don't let that shame bring you down. I want you to turn that into innovative disruption, which is the ability to recognise that this feels uncomfortable for a reason. It's that reason you want to embrace and not the by-product feeling. Embrace it and own it, instead of fearing it. This is where you can impart your own power of choice.

> **You will experience shame, remorse, regret or anger. Choose to embrace the fact that you simply have something to learn, or unlearn, and that's okay.**

Shitty leadership has impacted on corporate culture across the world, and it's time to come together and do something about it. It's not about pointing fingers and blaming and shaming; it's about how we can look inside and change our behaviours. When done by the majority, this changes how corporate cultures are driven.

It's okay to feel these fears; you're not alone, and together we can figure out how to change things across the globe. But the questions that remain are these: are you willing to better understand what shitty leadership means? Are you willing to look inside and say, "Yes, I may have displayed these behaviours, I will accept that," and are you open to becoming a more authentic and active leader? Are you willing to choose kindness over being right?

REFLECTIVE QUESTIONS

› What holds you back from accepting vulnerability as a strength?
› What drives your fear in the workplace?
› If you could change one choice you made recently, what would that be and why?
› Reflect on a time when you could have chosen to be more kind?

FOUR

"It is not my place to judge any person's beliefs, but choose rather to celebrate their ability to believe." — Tom Althouse

Don't Shoot The Messenger

Right now, there is a chance that you might be feeling a bit defensive. That may be your current choice. If so, proceed with caution. Be aware that how you're feeling might be a sign of something deeper.

A couple of weeks after I ran a workshop on this content, I was contacted by a member of the team who hadn't actually been at the workshop. She said she'd like to give me some feedback, and I happily agreed. Her feedback was as follows: "Everyone loved the course. They thought it was very reflective and very insightful. The only thing is, a couple of people commented that you came across a bit egocentric."

I appreciated her feedback, but I did push back a little. "Help me understand how that's feedback," I said.

"What do you mean?" she replied.

"Well," I said, "what you've actually just provided, seeing as you weren't in the room, is opinion." It's opinion because it's not connected to a direct action that I could change. It's simply how I was perceived that was passed on to you. Feedback would have sounded more like, "You interrupted people constantly," or "This particular exercise seemed to take longer than necessary." Those are things I can improve upon. Opinion is how I 'came across,' which, in my experience, has just as much, if not more, to do with how you're feeling than how I'm actually behaving.

Could it be that when people start to reflect and make the connection that they might have done some shitty leading, they get a little defensive?

Some people will accept, reflect and recognise their own behaviours; they'll say, "Okay, I'm going to move towards awareness and forge ahead."

Other people might have a defensive response: "Who the hell do you think you are, saying I'm a shitty leader?" Because sometimes, even the slightest perceived inference that you might be a shitty leader can create a tailspin of emotive or negative emotions. This is especially true of someone who may not yet be aware or ready to reflect on his or her shitty leadership behaviours. The natural, easy response is to say, "It's not me, it's you. How dare you infer that I'm a shitty leader? You're just egocentric!"

As a certified Life Coach, I'm not here to tell you or anyone how to live your life. I'm here to ask questions that will hopefully be thought-provoking and help you think of things differently, so that together we can uncover what you probably already know. It's about building your ability to demonstrate lens awareness. But when you're riddled with your own fear and shame, or when you think you 'don't do feelings', only to realise that you do (because everybody does), it becomes an eye-opener — and then you shoot the messenger (me!) because you don't want to deal with it (you).

It's natural to hide behind that pride because once you openly admit it, you can't take it back. She wasn't ready to do that. But what about you?

What you're feeling right now has nothing to do with me, or the person you're interacting with at that time, and everything to do with you. It has nothing to do with the people asking the questions; it's how you're choosing to perceive the question, or the impact you're feeling on what you're choosing to respond. Are you more insecure about a certain area? Then you're probably going to get defensive and make it about the messenger. That's just something to ponder. It's one of many potential lenses to consider.

PUSHING BACK: AN EXAMPLE

A while back, I was hired by a call centre to help fix their corporate culture. There were a lot of issues: the sales team were completely rogue and would sell products that hadn't yet been created; the back-office support teams lacked professional communications; the customer care department was run on hope and prayer. Managers would spend their days sitting at their desks eating, and no one bothered to interact with anyone else. The outbound contact centre handled inbound collection calls that were simply disastrous to hear. There was little internal support or comradery.

One of the leads was an overbearing, loud, boisterous individual who many feared simply because of his bark. He would loudly and publicly blame and shame if it meant making his point.

At one stage, I noticed that he had become rather distant with me. He was curt and short, and not as engaging as he had been previously. I approached him and asked if he could spare a few minutes, as I wanted to ask for some feedback. He accepted, and we went to a private place to chat.

I thanked him for his time before proceeding to seek clarity on the perceived distance I had been sensing. I asked if he could clear the air or provide any feedback about that. His response took me by surprise.

"Yes, I have been distant these last few weeks. You really pissed me off during the meeting where you said 'blank'. I intentionally pulled away, and I wanted you to feel it. I wanted you to know I was angry at you for what you said!"

I have to admit, I was floored. A senior leader wanted to teach me a lesson — so he acted like a child? This was the conduct of a senior executive of a rather large company? And he actually believed this was acceptable behaviour?

How many times have you been on the receiving end of this? How many times have you *treated others* like this?

I can practically hear my late mother laughing from beyond, reminding me to "use your words, Marky!" When did it become okay for a leader of any kind to take this attitude with another person, rather than simply communicating like an adult to clear the air, seek clarity, and engage in effective communications?

To make matters worse, his frustrations were based on a misperception. In the meeting he referred to, I had asked a question about a process, and someone else replied. It was the reply that made him angry, so it had absolutely nothing to do with me. It was his perception of my intent in asking the question. Unfortunately, he chose to believe what he had perceived. How quickly things could have been cleared up if he had simply talked to me.

But instead, he chose to engage in a childlike behaviour, vent to multiple people and exaggerate the events in the hope of smearing my reputation within the company. The ramifications of his behaviours added much unnecessary stress to his life and his staff, not to mention whomever else crossed his path over the same period. I wasn't pleased with it either and required some much needed personal and external venting time too — that was my choice.

The unfortunate truth is that this behaviour is quite normal for many adults. We've all been on the receiving end of counter-productive behaviours that originate from a misunderstanding or misperception. These types of behaviours, which usually stem from insecurity, can create a toxic corporate culture.

> **One person can, if permitted to do so, change an entire company from profitable and engaged, to profitable and *dis*engaged —which can easily develop into *un*profitable and disengaged.**

How you treat others and the choices you make as a leader support and promote both sales and service, and when those are done right the first time, with little to no rework, your company saves money. If your employees feel aligned, informed and valued, effective communications soar — and so does productivity. That is what a people-lens organisation feels like: treating people well, no matter what. That type of organisation doesn't tolerate or accept childlike behavioural choices from adults, because those poor behavioural choices instil toxicity in the workplace, incite disengagement across the company and reduce a sustainability approach to bottom line protection.

Shitty organisations run by shitty leadership are perceived as shitty organisations to work for. How do you want your organisation to be perceived?

WHAT'S BEHIND THE RESISTANCE?

A lot of the time, when I come across this kind of resistance to this content, I hear, "I don't do feelings." I've had plenty of men say things like, "Oh, are you going to talk about your feelings again, little girl?" Or, less hostile but no less misguided, "Oh Mark, I love everything you talk about, and it's great, but, you know, I'm not a chick." Yes, someone actually said that. Corporate misogyny at its finest, yes, and unfortunately so relevant to discuss in 2018.

There's a widespread misconception that being connected, wholehearted and showing vulnerability are exclusively female characteristics — and for some reason, these are perceived negatively.

If you're recognising that reaction in yourself, I challenge you to analyse it. First of all, why do those healthy expressions of emotion have to be labelled as characteristic of a certain gender? There's plenty of research to show that vulnerability and expressing emotion makes for healthier people, regardless of gender. Secondly, I think we need to consciously reorient our mindset if we believe that 'female' qualities are negative. That's unfounded and, to be frank, pretty unfair.

But regardless of your thoughts about sexism or gender, the fact remains that these qualities have no gender. We're not talking about 'feminine' leadership. We're talking about good leadership, leadership that makes for engaged employees and, ultimately, higher profits and happier employees. Don't let your aversion to 'feelings' get in the way of what's best for your company.

Then again, for a lot of leaders, this isn't a 'female' issue. It just feels wrong. They read our book or go to our workshops, and their response is something along the lines of, "This just goes against my grain. This doesn't feel like the way bosses are supposed to be."

Men and women alike succumb to this way of thinking. They believe they have to act in this traditional, almost parental style to get ahead. That kind of style is really based on a hierarchy — and it's a parent/child hierarchy. It's not even a modern parent/child hierarchy. It's from days long past, when children were supposed to be seen and not heard, and obey without question. It's authoritarian leadership, and someone who's been steeped in that for their whole career will naturally baulk at our ideas — even if they know they've shown some of these shitty leadership behaviours. They feel sort of ambivalent about that because it's ingrained in them; "This really is the way it's supposed to be." But that's not what the profit margins say.

Then again, many executives like this baulk at these ideas simply because they don't care. They're five years away from retirement and they think, *"Why should I bother?"* They've held this role for years, so experience tells them they must be doing it well — they got there, didn't they? Why should they start reflecting on it now?

The problem with this kind of thinking is that *you don't know what you don't know*. Sure, your behaviours so far have got you into this senior leadership role, but that doesn't mean it was best for the company. It could just mean that shitty leadership breeds shitty leadership. What about your company's growth? What about your bottom line? If you've never tried reflecting and growing in this way, you haven't seen how this methodology can grow your profits.

No matter how long you've been in your role, and no matter how close you are to retirement, changing your behaviour can make a long-term difference for your company. It can prepare your team for succession — who's taking over after you leave? How can you take your company to an even higher level in your final years of employment? It certainly won't happen with shitty leadership.

But there's another group of people who have a hard time implementing these changes, and it's not the high-power executives. It's the middle managers. It that's you, you might be reading this right now and thinking, "*Well, sure, but how can I implement this if I can't get the higher-ups on board?*" As I touched upon at the start of this book, people say that you can't push water up a mountain. Water trickles downwards. But here's the thing: shitty leadership trickles downwards, too.

ERODING RESISTANCE

I understand this frustration. With any change initiative, it's always best to begin at the starting line. In the corporate world, when you get to top-level management, in most cases that means the shittiest of the shitty leaders. If we start in the middle, then those middle management leaders have a rough time. Some of the executives you want to convince have not been on the receiving end of corporate feedback for decades. What if they're an owner of the company?

If you read our first book, you know all about the concept of managing up. That's exactly where you have to start. Remember the two questions: how do you like to be led, and how do you like to receive feedback? The second one can apply to managing up, as well. Let's review this again as we did earlier.

To do this, signpost to the executive that you'd like to provide them with some constructive feedback. Then ask:

› Would they be open to it?
› How would they like to receive it?

If they say no, you can always deliver it anyway. If they fire you, great — you don't have to work for a shitty leader anymore! All right, that's partially a joke. But you can always start by asking if they're open. Just say, "The next time we meet, would you be open to me providing some feedback? I want us to have the optimal working relationship." If they say no, well, you know they are a massively shitty leader, and you should probably find a new job. But if they say yes, you've got yourself an opportunity.

Then again, if you're the one who's resisting this — if you're the one who's reading this right now and feeling defensive — that's okay. Defensiveness means there's room for growth. Defensiveness is a sign of that innovative disruption: you're going to feel uncomfortable. You might feel threatened. But use it, lean into it and embrace the change.

Reflect. Take a deep breath and recognise that you might be feeling any combination of shame, anger, or frustration. Take a minute and ask yourself *why* you're feeling that way. There's a reason for it. Did you innately react that way, or did you choose to react that way? If it happened innately, then that's your predisposed tape, which says a lot, too. Where does that come from? How can you understand that more fully? Because, in my experience, the more you are against this stuff, the more you probably need it.

RECAP

A lot of the time, leaders are in positions of leadership because they trust their guts — they've made instinctive decisions, and it's served them well. How can you recognise when you actually need to change, if your gut is telling you that you don't?

The answer is simple: if you're reflecting honestly and authentically, you will recognise when you use your 'gut' as an excuse. You'll know. Whether you choose to act on that is up to you. Are you willing to remove the mask and make changes?

There are many reasons why people baulk at these lessons, and you might be experiencing any one of them. You've been in your position for decades, and this new stuff just doesn't feel right. Or you think your company is doing fine, so if it 'ain't broke', why fix it?

Are you sure it's not broken? Are you sure you have no room to grow? Is there no way your performance could improve at all?

For those who are really, truly, struggling with feeling empathy here, try thinking back to a time in your life when you felt your lowest. When you felt shamed, stupid or inadequate. Somewhere along the line, I suspect, upon reflection, you may realise that you still believe it.

If that's the case, pull back from your reflections and decide on one thing to empathise with yourself about.

REFLECTIVE QUESTIONS

› Put yourself in your own shoes, but in the past. How can you show empathy to that person?
› Who are the people that are in your inner-circle? Who are you closest to? How do they feel about you? Do your family members think you're a bully, but because you're so loud and boisterous, no one's ever had the heart to tell you? Reflect on that.
› Are you the same at work as you are at home, or is there a difference? If there is, reflect on why that difference is there.

FIVE

"I'm not scared to be seen, I make no apologies, this is me!"
— *'This Is Me', Soundtrack, The Greatest Showman*

Dealing with Shame

At this point, you've recognised some past behaviours that you might not be feeling great about. You're feeling the innovative disruption. You're feeling uncomfortable, but you've decided to keep reading — you want to move through this discomfort. In order to do that, we need to spend some time talking about one feeling that can be particularly toxic: shame.

When we feel shame, we put up all kinds of walls; we might respond with anger, silence, depression, or fear — but these are all rooted in shame. The encouraging thing to remember is that you're not alone in this: we all feel shame at one point or another. Unfortunately, it's natural. The danger is when we try to numb it. It can be incredibly tempting to just ignore shame, to refuse to deal with it healthily, to do anything at all in order *not* to feel it. The problem is, you can't pick and choose which feelings you numb. If you numb one, you numb them all. Which isn't healthy — and it isn't good for leadership.

When you recognise that you may have demonstrated certain behaviours, which have incited counterproductive actions and feelings in others, shame may become a by-product of your reflections. In innovative disruption, this is one of those moments when you can choose to *embrace* how this feels. Own it; that's the only way to move forward and fix things. You are the key to reducing the global epidemic of shame and shitty leadership that exists today.

PERSONALITY VS BEHAVIOUR

Often, when we make a mistake, we aren't told we've *done* something bad; we're told that we *are* something bad. That's a horrifying conclusion. Is it right or fair for anyone to be defined forever by their past actions? Is it productive? Definitely not. A mistake is just that: a mistake. You are not defined by it.

If you're feeling shame for past behaviours right now, you can rest assured that *those behaviours do not define you*. You can change, and you can grow; but if you hold on to shame for too long, it will debilitate you.

When we believe that we *are* something bad as a result of that overwhelming shame, it can close us off from accepting any form of positivity from anyone else. It can stop us from healing or growing. That paralysing kind of shame prevents actions that lead to positive change. It does nothing to help you graduate as a non-shitty leader.

Shame is natural, and we all feel it. But it does not define you; you are better than your past behaviours. Accepting that and moving past your shame is the most important step towards becoming a better leader — and perhaps even a happier and more content person.

EMBRACE LEARNING TO BECOME A NON-SHITTY LEADER

Dr Brené Brown makes an important distinction when it comes to shame. She describes healthy shame as *guilt*. In her TED2012 talk "Listening to Shame," she pointed out the following:

> "Shame is a focus on self, guilt is a focus on behaviour. Shame is "I am bad." Guilt is "I did something bad"... There's a huge difference between shame and guilt. And here's what you need to know. Shame is highly, highly correlated with addiction, depression, violence, aggression, bullying, suicide, and eating disorders. And here's what you need to know even more. Guilt is inversely correlated with those things. The ability to hold something we've done or failed to do up against who we want to be is incredibly adaptive. It's uncomfortable, but it's adaptive."

As we've said a few times, this is what innovative disruption is all about. That discomfort you're feeling? Embrace it! Use it to adapt, to grow, to take the steps you need to take to be better. Because you're fully capable of taking those steps. Don't let shame paralyse you. Embrace that guilt, and make the changes you need to make.

If you picked up a musical instrument that you'd never touched before, even if you loved it, you'd still be pretty shitty at it. You've never had lessons! If somebody said, "Oh, you're such a shitty musician," you'd probably just laugh and say, "Yes, I'm in the process of learning. I'm new. I need experience." It wouldn't put you on the defensive because you haven't made 'musician' a key part of your identity yet.

Then again, somebody that has been teaching guitar for 40 years would probably *identify* as a musician, even if they were shitty. Once you get into that identity thing, that's when it really feels personal. It's hard to grow or receive feedback if you're just operating under the belief that you are the best, you are a musician, and anyone who says otherwise is wrong. You've got to release that identity in order to grow. It's scary when our identity is threatened, but remember that you are more than your role. Don't let your white-knuckled grip on your idea of yourself as leaders keep you from learning and growing. Let it go, and that's when the develop opportunities begin.

LEAVING SHAME BEHIND: A PERSONAL JOURNEY

During my late 20s and early 30s, I was morbidly obese, as I talked about in Book One and mentioned earlier. What's more, I was also in extremely bad, self-inflicted debt. At the time, my partner and I had good jobs, owned a car each and our own condominium and took regular holidays. Our friends considered us affluent, and I never corrected their misperceptions — I liked how it felt.

I spent many years of my life in work roles that I didn't particularly enjoy because I didn't have a choice. My debt was too high. I tried applying for other jobs but wasn't hired. At times, it felt like I was drowning. I would go home and eat more, and then I would go and spend money to feel better, not realising that I was feeding my own problem. There was a lot of shame going on, but I wasn't able to recognise it until much later in life.

Finally, I can comfortably share that story because I've moved past it. But for years, I never shared it with anyone. I was too ashamed. I liked how people thought I was more affluent than I really was. I liked how it felt because it was the opposite of the dark truth. Now, I own it. I'm not ashamed of it, instead I've chosen to simply own my truth.

I had to lead myself before I could lead others. I had to take the initiative to get out of that hole. Once you can do that, leading others is the natural next step.

A lot of leadership books and talks out there are all about what you do for others. That's an important part of leadership, definitely, but if you're only focusing on that, you're missing the foundation.

Great leadership *starts* with what you do for yourself.

In the same TEDTalk about shame, Dr Brown calls empathy, "the antidote to shame...Shame needs...secrecy, silence and judgement" to grow. In other words, if you embrace it, own up to it, and then receive empathy, you can really start to grow past shame and let it go. Empathy flies in the face of the notion that we don't deserve connections or love.

Can you remember a time when you empathised with someone; particularly someone who was feeling ashamed? How much better was that situation because of your empathy? It makes a world of difference. It breaks down walls. It promotes growth. It is, as Dr Brown says, the antidote to shame.

My challenge to you today is to empathise with *yourself*.

RECAP

Shame is a toxic emotion, one that can paralyse us and stop us from growing. It stems from the lie that your past behaviours define your identity. Shitty leadership is behaviour, not a personality trait, and shitty leaders are not bad people. If you're feeling shame, you're not alone — almost everyone feels something like that at this point in the journey. The key is to use that feeling to improve and to grow — not to allow it to stop you in your tracks.

REFLECTIVE QUESTIONS

› In Book One, you were asked to write a letter to your past self. If you did this, read it again, and if not, write one now.
› Reflect on a time when you should have been more empathetic to yourself. We can be really hard on ourselves; we beat ourselves up without realising it. Reflect on this time and work through how you can forgive yourself.
› Determine why you chose this behaviour. What's different now?

SIX

Recap of The Ego Continuum

Misperceptions can run rampant when poor behaviours are the cornerstone of an interaction. This chapter will review the Ego Continuum concept, which is essential to understanding the next step in your growth. As you read on, focus on understanding the differences between the way you see yourself and the way others see you. This understanding, the understanding of the Ego Continuum, will prepare you for active, non-shitty leadership in the context of empathetic interactions.

WHAT IS THE EGO CONTINUUM?

The Ego Continuum is an awareness framework that teaches you how to bring awareness of how you are perceived at work alongside how you see yourself. This continuum has *insecurity* to the left and *narcissism* to the right. Don't think

The Ego Continuum

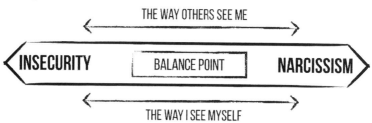

Your leadership brand zone surrounds your balance point and is where you work from best.

of this as a straight line; think of it as a circle. The points of insecurity and narcissism actually converge, because those two qualities can appear very similar, or they are similar to perceive and misperceive. Between those points is the way others see you — versus the way you see yourself. If you stand in the middle of that continuum, you're at what we call your balance point. That's the place to stay. This can also feel like a bit of a crossroads.

Insecurity and narcissism drive shitty leadership behaviours. We all know that, sometimes, our insecurities incite choices in us that are far from sensitive, but narcissism can be even more problematic — because narcissistic behaviours are often rewarded in organisations. Interestingly enough, narcissists are rife in many corporations; politics and sports are two other areas that seem to be driven by narcissistic behaviours. Decisive, strong-willed leadership is often attractive in these environments. Narcissists get things done, but often at the expense of their employees or team.

Imagine that you're standing at your balance point, where you work from your best you. Based on where you are on that continuum, the lens of how others see you versus how you see yourself will differ. If you start to veer towards insecurity, people can misperceive you as vulnerable, kind, soft, timid, anxious, negative, doubtful, uncertain, self-loathing, or self-deprecating. Notice how the words can be perceived positively and negatively? That's the point. If you start down the path towards narcissism, those misperceptions might sound more like determined, strong, courageous, commanding, bossy, pushy, rude, arrogant, vain or self-righteous.

How we are perceived is in the eye of the perceiver and will correlate to their own ego continuum position and lens.

Unbranded leaders, or those who've not declared who they are, are at risk of being misperceived often. In most disengaged workplace cultures, this is where shitty leadership perception is born.

The first step here is to gain some insight into yourself and your past behaviours. Reflect on interactions where you felt disconnected, misread or misunderstood. Were you being perceived incorrectly? Why do you think that was? The continuum will provide a balance point, where the way others see you and the way you see yourself are a bit closer together. If they're not and the perceiver has completely misperceived it all, if you've shared your leadership brand and led from a place of humility, the impacts of the misperceptions are gravely reduced, and recovery begins.

You can protect and manage those perceptions while at your balance point by working inside your leadership brand zone. This is an imaginary zone that serves as an account of all that you declare to be as a leader. It reduces potential misperceptions and proactively declares the leader you are. Your ability to remain self-aware helps to control the placement of your leadership brand zone, which is completely fluid along the continuum.

YOUR LEADERSHIP BRAND

Somewhere on this continuum is your leadership brand, spanning between insecurity and narcissism. Your job, when you create your leadership brand, is to plot on the continuum where your balance point is — and how far to the left and right you tend to go. That way, you can openly declare that there will be times where you will, for example, show strength — and perhaps need to be perceived as a dictator — because sometimes you'll have to say, "I just need you to do it."

Give your team a heads up about this; letting them know that hey, you're not trying to be rude, you're just trying to get things done. This helps mitigate stress or misperceptions because you've told everyone ahead of time. The declaration doesn't give license for you to be rude, it just allows you to proactively communicate to mitigate potential misperceptions before they occur. Your staff will notice and appreciate the effort. Proactive.

It's when you step outside of your leadership brand and demonstrate behaviours that are not part of what you've declared, you enter the land of misperceptions, and are potentially then perceived differently, or as a shitty leader. You've created dissonance; a sort of psychological white noise. And that's where the shame comes from because ultimately, it's easier to complain about someone than not to.

As important as this is, a word of caution: don't go into that shame spiral because people are misperceiving you. Don't base all of your actions on what others might think. It's not necessarily about what they think of you — it's about *how you connect with them*, to lead more effectively.

When you start to make this about them and their needs instead of your own, you can look at it through their lens.

What behaviours are you demonstrating that they might see differently? You think you are strong, but maybe you're a bit of an ass. Do you want to be strong, or do you want to be an ass? What do you need to do differently to change this perception? If you've chosen to be an ass, then congratulations, you've succeeded, but you'll also need to own the outcomes.

It can be that simple. It's about them, not you.

That's the beginning of active leadership.

THE THREE PILLARS OF ACTIVE LEADERSHIP

As we discussed in Book One, there are three main components forming active leadership. First is self-awareness, second is leadership brand, and last is effective feedback delivery. In its simplest form, active leadership is where the leader spends at least 50% of their time with their staff. This could be spent coaching, one-on-one, training, casually delivering feedback, a formal review, discussing goals, objections, or issues. Sometimes, it's just to check in to see how they are feeling.

If you're not focusing at least 50% of your time as a leader on your staff like this, they may perceive you as demonstrating shitty leadership behaviour, or as being an inactive leader. I know that some of you may be thinking, *"How can I spend that much time with my staff when I have all my other work to do?"* This is a question worth asking. How are you going to do this? Assume from here that this is what is expected of you. You need to find a way to make it work. This isn't tough love; it's reality. Leaders usually have a lot on their plates and must use exceptional time management and organisational skills. You want to be less of a shitty leader, don't you? So, stop whining about it and keep reading.

Being an active leader is what drives change. It's what builds consistency and establishes rules. Some employees will cut corners and take advantage when they can if they don't respect you as a leader, or the job. You have to teach them to care. How are you supposed to do this? By giving them an environment to care about. If your staff isn't in an environment they care about, they won't go above and beyond to meet the needs of the customer. They won't solve customer's problems, and that impacts on the bottom line. Active leadership drives a culture of engagement. We can start to reduce and eliminate your disengaged workforce to become a more productive one.

Think back to the three pillars; self-awareness, leadership brand and effective feedback delivery. Once you become self-aware, you start to recognise who you are. You start to put that on paper, and that becomes the process of creating your leadership brand. That's how you avoid the misperceptions. That's how you can declare who you are and the type of leader you want to be, the type of leader you aspire to be, and what working with you and for you means — so that your employees can hold you accountable.

Then, in order to drive change and remove the disengaged workforce, according to your leadership brand, you've got to be delivering feedback in the way that is best for those individuals. If you have 15 employees, then, potentially, you need to deliver feedback in 15 different ways. You cater your feedback delivery style to suit the needs of your employees. That's making it about them, not about you. At the end of the day, that's what drives and reduces a disengaged workforce.

Maintaining these three components — self-awareness, leadership brand and effective feedback delivery — is the key to successful active leadership.

RECAP

The Ego Continuum is a framework to understand and mitigate how your team perceives or misperceives your behaviours and actions. Understanding how you're perceived is important not for your own benefit or 'popularity,' but so that you can more successfully connect with your team, demonstrate active leadership and develop an engaged workforce. Active leadership is made up of three pillars: self-awareness, leadership brand and effective feedback delivery. Maintaining those three components as well as finding your balance point on the Ego Continuum is the most healthiest, most effective way to lead your team successfully.

REFLECTIVE QUESTIONS

› Where do you plot yourself on the ego continuum?

SEVEN

The Shadows You Cast

Shitty leadership, more than any other factor, contributes to toxic workplace culture. The higher up the leader, the more they have the power to affect that toxicity. But you'll never be able to change your leadership if you aren't aware of it. Wherever you go, you're casting shadows, and those shadows can be positive or negative. It's up to you. But, again, the only way you'll be able to change it is if you are truly self-aware.

To change your leadership and create a healthy workplace culture, you have to first be aware of the shadows you cast.

ORIGINS OF COMPANY CULTURE

Where does the culture of a company originate? If you are a 9-to-5 company, Monday to Friday, then at 5 o'clock on Friday, everybody goes home. No one is there until 9 o'clock

Monday morning. Over the weekend, when the building is empty, what's the company culture like? There isn't one, of course. It's void.

The people establish the culture. The leaders guide the people, which means the leaders will guide the culture. The higher up you are, the more your behavioural outputs will link back to that culture. This creates a uniformed approach to looking at and understanding what culture even means.

A while back, I was hired as a consultant to work in a contact centre. They swore blindly that they were a 'people culture.' Upon my observations, they lost clients due to a lack of communication. They lost clients because sales were disconnected to the rest of the business, they sold products that didn't exist, and they expected the rest of the business to pick it up and figure out how to make it work. They had multiple senior leaders with different strategies and leadership style approaches.

They were a sales-driven culture that provided a level of service that was enough to create some sustainability, but not enough, through my lens, to be considered a true 'people' culture. When you set people up to fail just so you can make a sale, you're not really upholding a culture or movement that supports people.

Now, I understand how business works. I understand that if you don't have sales, you don't have a business. But it is also true that if you sell something right the first time, there is no additional rework, which means there is no negative impact on the client. Their risk of cancelling diminishes greatly and their impact on sustainability and client retention increases. This approach also reduces or eliminates rework, which retains a greater portion of your profits.

There is something to be said for doing it right the first time. If your profit margin is 30%, but you have to do three versions of rework, you've killed that 30%. Whereas if you're honest with the customer and say, "Listen, we can't do this until this timeframe," then you set yourself up to deliver that product right when you actually deliver it. If you can't convince a client to do it right the first time, then I would question how effective your salespeople really are! Proactive and effective leadership is external too.

Every time you make that effort, you are closer to retaining that customer. The problem is that people don't generally look at it that way. They look at it through their own department's lens, and feel slighted. Sales get blamed for this, service gets blamed for that, and a level of animosity develops. This contributes to toxic workplace culture; it all links together.

A people culture means you have to really put *people* first. Unfortunately, you often get companies who say, "We can't afford to hire these people; we have to really, really buckle down." Then you walk by the boardroom every second Thursday and see the senior executives with a catered lunch. Mixed messages add to negative perceptions.

Most senior leaders rarely think outside of themselves, and when they do, they're thinking about profit margins and their annual bonus. They're not thinking about how their employees are people that they should be first. They're thinking about how the employee can put the boss first by helping with their bonus.

> **The leaders create the culture. What culture are you creating?**

WHAT ARE THE SHADOWS YOU CAST?

Part of recognising your brand is learning how to become self-aware and understanding how you're perceived. The shadows you cast can be identified in the feedback forms you provide. This is especially true if you have an honest crew, or if you have maintained confidentiality, so that employees feel safe giving you truthful feedback without fear of retaliation. This process can help you learn what you're leaving behind.

If you're a productive, fair leader and competent at delivering feedback, then you will leave behind an air of equality and support. If you are a shitty leader, you will find that you're leaving behind a path of fear, toxicity, frustration and apathy. If this is the case, you clearly have some work to do. As you're learning about effective feedback delivery and asking your staff how they prefer to receive it, you can also simply ask them for their thoughts. Engage in your own vulnerability and declare that you're trying to become more self-aware as a leader. Ask if they have any feedback for you and see how they respond.

You can also find some quiet time and use reflective exercises to think back on past experiences. Reflect on times when you upset your staff or felt frustrated, despairing or isolated at work. These heightened times can manifest in what I like to call our 'shitty moments,' when we have no intention of being a shitty leader, but our behaviour indicates otherwise. Regardless of the method you choose, be willing to look inside yourself to understand, once and for all, how to take back control and truly inspire others through active non-shitty leadership.

As you begin this journey of self-awareness, you need to recognise the term 'perception management.' At all times, as a leader, you're being watched. Though not necessarily always in a negative or malicious way, there certainly can be some who are looking for the first opportunity to catch us out. It sounds cynical, but it's very true.

When we walk, most of us are looking forward so that we don't bump into things. However, you need to be looking behind you as well. When you have an interaction, no matter what it is, you need to be aware of how you're coming across.

Years ago, I worked for a certain company, and my role meant that I was very busy. Every single day, I had back-to-back meetings. My only downtime was walking through the corridors, in between those meetings. I would walk and look forward, but not see anything other than focusing on where my next meeting was.

People would pass by and acknowledge me. They would try to have conversations. Apparently, I would be completely cold and turned off. The perception was that I was a bit unapproachable. *Mark's rude. Mark's not engaging. I said hi to Mark, and he ignored me.* This went on for a short period of time, and then finally someone said something to me and I realised what I was doing. I had to go back and do damage control.

I wasn't trying to be disrespectful to anyone. I was just so focused that I couldn't see what was happening. The shadows I was casting were negative, even though that was not my intention. All it took to change that was a bit of feedback and then my own self-awareness.

In my early days of being a team manager, I was also easily distracted. I would be on my phone during one-on-one sessions. My ADD had set in, and I wasn't able to control it, which was the excuse I used. People would feel offended, and for a good reason: they felt that I wasn't listening to them, even though I was trying my best. It just wasn't working. I had to find coping strategies.

When I go into meetings now, I'm very aware of my phone. I make sure it's either not on the desk, or turned face-down, on silent. I make sure that I sit away from any distractions. I don't face the door or an outside window. I try to sit in the direct eye line of the person I'm talking to, and I make sure I focus on their eyes. Those are the tricks for engagement, which allow me to cast the right shadows.

Never forget: you are always casting shadows. No matter what you do, you're casting shadows with your leadership. Shadows can be dark and foreboding, or they can provide shade on a hot day. You have the power to make your shadows a blessing or a curse to those around you. But to control that, you have to be aware of it. If you're not aware, you can't do anything about it.

The shadows we cast as leaders make a huge difference to our team. Just think about your current leader and the shadows they cast. How do these feel? What do the shadows incite within you? Do they contribute to your current culture's toxicity?

RECAP

How are you contributing to your current toxic workplace culture? Start by trying to gain an understanding from your employees of what shadows you're casting. If you're casting a negative shadow, you're probably one of the catalysts of that toxic culture. That toxicity is a result of the things that you or your fellow leaders are doing. And there's a consequence to that.

The good news is that you can prevent that consequence; you can instigate change. But you have to be aware, first and foremost, of the shadows you cast.

EIGHT

Self-Awareness Awareness

Frequency: your ability to focus on not allowing triggers to impact on your thinking, behaviours, actions, feelings or relationships in negative ways.

We don't know what we don't know, but when we become aware of our own awareness, we can control our reactions.

> **When you let someone make you feel like shit, it's important to remember just that: *you let them*.**

You allowed it. You have the power to control what you say and how you feel, which means that if you have a shitty leader, it doesn't have to control your every waking minute. It doesn't have to impact on your physical and mental health to the point of exhaustion. You can alter your lens. Keep reading.

BEING AWARE OF THE NEED FOR SELF-AWARENESS

We hear about it all the time in self-help books and lectures at work, but how much do you actually know about what self-awareness means — and how it's linked to becoming less of a shitty leader?

Self-awareness is defined as the conscious knowledge of our character, feelings, motivation and desires. It means being cognizant of who you are, what you say, how you say it, and understanding how the things you say might be perceived by the individual receivers. Self-awareness is being mindful of what you leave behind when you walk away; like the shadows you cast. It is being conscious of the impact that you are having on people, especially those you should be actively leading.

Where are you on the Ego Continuum? Do you sound condescending and patronising when you're supposed to be supportive and inspiring? What if you're giving feedback to an employee you don't personally like? Can they sense that you don't like them? How aware of self are you? If you're not self-aware, perhaps you're demonstrating characteristics that could be deemed shitty leadership behaviours. Perhaps its these demonstrated characteristics that influence others and their potential misperceptions? How would you know, if you're not self-aware?

Are you self-aware enough to know you're self-aware? Because if you ask anybody, "Are you self-aware?" They're going to say, "Yeah, of course I am."

Okay, then. How do you know?

I know because I am aware of my behaviour. I'm aware of my surroundings. I'm aware of my mood, which then can be linked back to frequency. I'm aware of what I may or may not be portraying. I'm aware of my audience. I'm aware that I'm being aware.

Not always, of course, but I try my very best to be aware that I'm aware. When I start to feel myself responding emotionally, getting upset or allowing counterproductive workplace behaviours, that's my red flag. That's my reminder to back up, look around and ask myself what's going on. What's happening? How can I course correct? This is when I check in with my frequency.

Self-awareness is not just for you. It's also essential for managing up: for dealing with shitty leaders. You don't have to let shitty leaders define your life. If you can be aware of yourself, your reactions, your triggers, your own impacts, then you can begin to balance your own frequency.

BALANCING YOUR FREQUENCY

Imagine your frequency is your road of focus. Visualise an actual road. Your task is to remain on this road at all times; it runs right through the centre of your leadership brand zone. As we mentioned before, your leadership brand zone is where you work from your best self. It keeps your staff comfortable, and it's where you feel you're most grounded. It's how you define your external leadership style and needs.

There are times when staying on this road will be difficult. One of those times is when the 'energy vampires' come to visit. They suck the life force from you, leaving you feeling drained, tired, angry, bitter or just in a shitty mood. This is when you are most at risk of stepping outside your leadership brand into the land of misperceptions — and in return, being perceived as a shitty leader.

However, these energy vampires are not always evil. Sometimes they're unaware that they're even vampires. They have become so comfortable in their own chaos that they don't realise (or choose not to realise) how that chaos is affecting them.

These are the people that you feel exhausted after a one-minute chat. The ones who always want to talk, or seek advice that they never seem to follow. They are the perpetual victims: "*Oh, poor me. Oh, why does this always happen to me?*" They are the self-deprecating, low self-worth, constant complainers amongst us.

What they don't realise is that those are their *chosen* behaviours.

By choosing to remain on your frequency road, you can end the external blame game and take complete responsibility for retaining your focus. You don't allow yourself to take the bait, and you remain in control of you. You proactively protect your energy when a vampire comes for a feed, simply by being aware. Rather than succumbing to their powers, you firmly plant yourself on your road and change your lens to your newfound awareness. In this way, you're able to focus on what they're saying, *without accepting the emotional connection that goes along with it*. When that connection is made, you've opened an energy vein. Then, that energy vampire starts to feed, depleting you of your natural energy or frequency.

Remember that no one can make you feel anything. "Oh, he makes me so angry!" Does he really? How does someone *make* you feel something? Are you not choosing to feel that?

We are not defined by what happens to us. We are defined by how we choose to handle it. If someone slaps you across the face, you feel pain because it is a physical contact that's sending stimuli to your brain. Words? Words don't hurt. It's how you perceive the content and intonation that hurts.

It's all about how we choose to assimilate data. If we are in our Negative Nelly mindset, for example, if we're having a bad hair day, or feel bloated because we ate sweets at lunch and are angry at ourselves because now we have to do an extra 40 minutes on the treadmill — if we allow ourselves to be affected, then anything and everything in life will lead us off our frequency.

Stress is, ultimately, a choice. People often say to me, "You're so on the go. You've got so much to do. How are you not stressed?"

The answer is because I choose not to be. I reflect on this many times a day.

That being said, it's not always easy. I am a snap of the fingers away from being Mr Negative. I've just learned to control it because I've found my frequency. I've developed coping strategies for remaining on my frequency and not letting those energy vampires steal my energy. I've decided not to let anyone do that to me anymore.

One example of these coping strategies: I have conversations with myself. I talk to myself when I'm driving my car. People must think I'm singing — or that I'm just nuts. But you know what? I like having conversations with me! I can get truly real with myself. I don't lie to myself anymore.

I will say stuff like, "Oh Mark — you were such an ass in that meeting today. You really wanted to be right. What's the damage control? What do you need to do? Tomorrow you must do this..."

Or something like, "Wow, you did really well today. That was really good." Why was it good? Because I stayed on my frequency and I didn't let that silly nonsense pull me into that argument. I didn't take the bait. I chose to be kind, and it actually made a difference. I do laugh at myself most days and have found it helps with keeping the ego in check, which supports the 'kindness over being right' mentality.

If I'm stressed, I talk to myself, too. "*This is happening!*" And then I respond: "*Oh, shut the hell up. Seriously, look at all the things you've accomplished. Look at where you are today. Look at what you're in the process of doing. Suck it up, move on. Go home, have a doughnut, do some exercise, have a coffee, watch a bit of TV. You'll be fine, believe me. The world will keep spinning.*"

Then I'll laugh at myself for getting caught up in my own unnecessary drama. I could cope negatively by eating really bad food, or choosing to be stressed out completely; not sleeping, tossing and turning all night — but the truth is, I don't need to be doing that. What is the truth? Why did I get upset?

People might think I'm wacky, but I honestly find it amusing. It works! I've found my frequency, and I'm going to do *whatever it takes* to keep myself there — no matter who thinks I'm odd. Odd is awesome, by the way. Try it.

> **It's about frequency alignment, frequency awareness, and then: frequency ownership.**

When you wake up in the morning and you're in a bad mood, be aware of the fact that you're choosing to be in that bad mood. No one has done that to you. You just woke up in a shitty mood. Where are you on the road? Where are you in your leadership brand? See it, own it, fix it.

Figure out why you're in a shitty mood and get back to the right frequency. Be thankful that you woke up at all. Find the positive in something that gives you the courage to get out of bed; choose the frequency you know you should be on.

This one time I had a houseguest, and we worked together. Every day, all I did was vent. While we worked together, I would vent and vent and vent, because I was tired of working with shitty leaders. I was just tired.

I had internally quit, but physically stayed. I needed the money (I wanted the money). I was biding my time until something new came along. I was caught in a spiral of venting on a regular basis. It got to the point where I started to feel like crap physically. I was tired. I didn't go to the gym.

One day, the houseguest — a person who never normally talked back or spoke abrasively in any way — turned to me and said, "Mark, I have to stop you. You're driving me nuts. Shut up. If you don't want to do this job anymore, then you should give your effing notice and leave. Enough with the whining, I don't want to hear it anymore!"

The fact that this kind of reaction was so out of character for her was, in all honesty, my wake-up call.

Around the same time, I went to a self-awareness workshop that opened my eyes to the whole concept of frequency. Frequency means focusing on what matters. If you have a goal, do you think it's better to spend time thinking about that goal, or whining about your shitty boss?

Part of this is the value of visualisation. If I have a specific goal — say, to start a business — I need to focus on that goal. I need to visualise it because then I start to do things that focus my attention on what I need to do to get there. I don't let the small things bother me. I don't get caught up in venting. I surround myself with people who want to pull me up and not tear me down. The right people.

My behaviours drive my end goal of starting a business. That visualisation keeps me on track. It's not just simply a case of, 'think about your business and it will magically happen'. It's about setting your own frequency to start doing your work with an aligned focus on how to achieve your goals. It's not allowing your procrastination to flourish or make excuses through the behaviours of others.

Think of it as the frequency of a radio station. If you move the dial to the left or right, you're going to hear white noise. If you keep your radio station on 98.5 because that's your frequency, you'll hear quality music. Deviate to 98.1, 98.3 or 98.7, and it's not going to work. It's going to be white noise or garbled voices. The only thing energy vampires and those unnecessary distractions need to catch you is that white noise.

Each of us controls the radio dial to tune into our own right frequency. In fact, you're the only one who can control it. No one puts you in a bad mood. You put yourself in a bad mood because you choose to think like that. I can't tell you how many times I talk myself off the ledge these days; you have to be self-aware to find your frequency and make sure that you're tuned into the right station.

TUNING AWAY FROM YOUR FREQUENCY

When practising self-awareness, there are a few red flags that let you know when you've fallen off your frequency. The most common are venting, whining, moaning, crying, yelling, screaming or even just complaining. When we respond to things from an emotive state that appear out of control, that's a big loss of frequency alignment.

Now, to clarify, I do think it's important in the workplace for every person to have a trusted 'vent.' Because at times, we all just need to blow off some steam. There's nothing wrong with that, as long as you can trust that person, and declare that you're venting. It doesn't normally require a response, feedback, or an opinion; it's usually just a case of getting something off your chest. Set a time limit, allow the vent, then move on.

> **The challenge then becomes: how do you self-vent? How do you talk *yourself* off the ledge?**

That's what we're talking about with self-awareness. Because what you'll find is that when you start to become self-aware, you self-soothe. You recover faster. You're not getting caught up in the drama. You're not getting comfortable in the chaos. You actually start to become uncomfortable in the chaos. You recognise when that chaos feeling is coming, and you take action to get rid of it. You stop and spot check, you express gratitude, and you move past it. "*This too shall pass.*"

On the other hand, if you move off your frequency, you'll keep feeling like crap. You'll just be in a bad mood and stay there; all day, all week, all year — all your life! A lot of people have developed behaviours where they actually feel more comfortable in that chaos, simply because change is difficult.

This leads us to emotional self-saboteurs. These are the folks who say one of two things:

"Things are going so well that, you know, something shitty is going to happen because things never work out for me."

"I might as well make it shitty now because it's just going to be shitty later. At least that way I'm still in control of it."

They don't even try. They're off their frequency.

I worked with a peer years ago that was a senior manager. She was one of the most grounded people I've ever worked with. She ended up mentoring me in adult learning; she believed in me at a time when I barely believed in myself. We were asked to lead this massive, massive project across the entire organisation, which involved training 4000 people over six months across the country, and this senior manager wanted me to spearhead it.

I learned so much. We had so many issues and challenges, but she always remained supportive. She was constantly asking me how she could help, encouraging me and telling me things like, "You got this!" She never allowed her feathers to be ruffled. I never saw her vent. She made you feel valued in a short amount of time. She was purely supportive; the epitome of the leader that I aspired to become. She was very self-aware and tuned into her frequency, and because of that, she was an excellent leader.

RECAP

The benefits of becoming self-aware don't just extend to your leadership — as a human being; awareness takes you to the next level. It's the start of that journey. When you accept that no one can *make* you feel anything, that your reactions and feelings are within your control, you can begin to tune into your own frequency. You can start to let go of stress and negativity and live your absolute best self as a leader and a person. Allowing others to 'make' you feel negative emotions just leaves you living in chaos, with less focus, less human connection and a lower sense of well-being.

Choosing your frequency, on the other hand — choosing your own reactions and emotional state — sets you into a life of peace, success, growth — and of leadership you can be proud of.

NINE

The How of Self-Awareness

Frequency balance is the authentic ability to know who you are and how you react to others, combined with an awareness and an ownership of the shadows you cast. But how exactly do you achieve this? There is a lot to explore in this chapter; we will discuss how to own and maintain our own energy, or, simply put, how to stop blaming others and taking responsibility for everything in our lives. This is how you find authenticity, and from there, a more effective leadership brand emerges.

TRIGGERS, FOCUS & PEOPLE

Let's talk a little bit about what a trigger is. A trigger is focused in either the workplace, the home or your personal life. It influences a reaction to a situation or an event based on behaviours, actions or the words of others. These can be perceived as emotional or emotive responses, but remember that there is a difference between showing emotion and reacting emotionally to things. An emotional response is not always negative.

If you are fuelled by being kind and don't just want to be right, you can release your past learned behaviours. You are the leader and your team need you. If they are wrong, does it make you feel better to point it out? If they have made an error, did they make it on purpose? Does this error make them less human? No one comes to work to do a bad job on purpose.

By choosing kindness, you retain humility and focus on the development required to help them not make the error again. This approach doesn't mean you ignore the error they made; it will naturally require a course correction. But you don't have to choose to be a shitty leader when helping them fix it or in the feedback delivery.

The first how of self-awareness is this: you have to understand your triggers and make sure you choose a different or more appropriate response.

Some examples of triggers might be:
› When you've held a door for someone who then chooses to not make eye contact and/or ignore you.
› People who lack spatial awareness in public — who might stop walking in the middle of a busy corridor without looking behind first. Think of this as them not checking their blind spot when driving.
› The customer service or retail advisor who doesn't make eye contact when you're waiting in a queue.
› Passive Aggressive behaviours — a type of behaviour or personality categorised by indirect resistance to the demands of others and an avoidance of direct interaction.

- People who constantly choose to be right over kind — those who need to validate or prove you're wrong just because. Reflect on why they want or need to be right.

Some workplace specific triggers may be:

- Employees who lie or demonstrate behaviours outside of your moral compass
- Employees who are unprofessional, rude or arrogant
- Employees who blame or shame, point fingers, ridicule, bully
- Employees who pass the buck and take no responsibility for their actions
- Employees who are argumentative or respond to situations emotionally or negatively

What are your common places or moments that incite your triggers?

- Work or specific places?
- People? Partners, children, family, co-workers?
- Crowds?
- Travelling (car, traffic, public transit)?
- When you're questioned or challenged — and by whom?

What are your workplace triggers, what are your home triggers and what are your personal triggers? Home and personal, of course, can often be tied together. When you are self-aware, as soon as you walk into the workplace, you should be leaving your home and personal triggers at the door. When you arrive at work, you need to turn your workplace frequency on and recognise your new triggers in that space. It might be that one person I work with constantly pushes my buttons. They might be harmless, but if I'm teetering on the side of my frequency and Billy comes up to me and says, "Hey, big guy, what's going on?" Well, at that point, I'm just done. I retaliate, and now I'm angry. The next one-on-one I go to, Susan gets a reaming that she didn't need, because Billy triggered me.

The reality is, however, that neither of these people are at fault — I am.

> **Because it's my responsibility to take responsibility for myself.**

At some point, I need to find Billy and say, "I'd very much appreciate if you would stop addressing me as big guy. It doesn't work for me, and I'd like it to stop. Whether it's humour or not, I don't like engaging in those kinds of interactions at work. I'd really appreciate it if you would stop doing that." I have also chosen my words and tone to suit Billy's preferred feedback delivery style that I learned from asking the two questions.

It's not about shaming Billy; it's about changing behaviour. Billy might be a peer. Billy might be senior to me. It doesn't matter. Billy is doing something that I don't like, and I don't want to be a part of. I don't need to be 'right' with Billy, to try to shame him, but I do need to tell him that I feel uncomfortable and how we can fix it respectfully.

To help yourself negotiate triggers, one tactic is to articulate these boundaries to those you expect to follow them. Then, all involved can take and accept responsibility for that boundary. Whatever your triggers are in the workplace, home, or personally, you have to set up your own boundaries to mitigate them, and you have to take responsibility for those boundaries. Boundaries setting equals effective communication. Don't assume your staff or peers know specifics about you and your behaviour without you having explicitly communicated. We sometimes expect people we work with (and family) to ~~read our minds.~~ We don't communicate effectively and then get upset when we don't get what we need or want. Have you communicated what you expect? Set the boundaries of what is acceptable before you expect alignment. Boundary setting is part of your focus.

We are responsible for how we are treated by others. If this doesn't match your boundaries, then you need to course correct. You need to take action. Setting boundaries is necessary, especially during times of confusion. Many times, we assume the boundaries are understood when they're not. We assume everyone thinks and reacts the same way as we do. Clarification comes in very handy here. For example, Billy may have assumed that calling me 'big guy' was fine since he's done it for years and I laughed every time. I have also referred to myself in the same manner when out for a drink with the team. To Billy, it was perfectly acceptable, because I engaged with it. If coach him now, after all these years, I'll look like a hypocrite, or that my silence meant consent. Manage accordingly, be clear and own it so that you're on the same page with a clear understanding of why.

To do this, you must assess whether you are situationally focused. Are you focused on the area you should be? Are you aware of your surroundings? Are you in the moment? If not, how can you obtain a more aligned focus on the areas that require development? Whether you're looking at your own development or the development of your team, how can you ensure that you're focused on the right areas? Take some time to work out when your focus tends to drift, and find out how you can keep it in check. Focus on being focused.

Take the time to understand who you're interacting with. Who is depleting your energy? What do they demonstrate that sets off your triggers? The people element helps you to align your focus, and that leads back to your trigger avoidance.

FEELINGS & CHOICES: FINDING YOUR BALANCE

Feelings and choices involve finding a balance. Why do we feel what we feel? When you're aligned with your frequency, you can more effectively manage how you feel and think.

Reflect for a moment on where your thoughts come from. Do they come from a situation? Are they planted in you by an outside source? No.

Our thoughts come from ourselves.

We all have thoughts, and we put these into our own heads. Sometimes we allow our thoughts to get the better of us, and this triggers an emotional response.

If you're driving and get stuck in traffic, do you lose your mind, or is it just one of those things? Are you late for work, or the theatre? The situation will affect your trigger. But, either way, is there any productivity in choosing to be angry at the traffic, and making yourself feel worse? Just learn to give yourself more travel time!

Adding frustration or anger affects approximately zero outcomes — it just makes you feel like crap. When you place the onus where it should be, the little things that used to trigger you become just that: little things that really don't matter. Traffic rage is a learned behaviour. It doesn't help with productivity or replenish your energy. In fact, at times like these, you become your own energy vampire! Why would you choose to do that to yourself?

Why do people react differently to the same situation? For example, if you're in a shop and you see a single parent looking completely embarrassed because their child is having a tantrum, you'll notice that some people will say, "Oh my, what a shitty parent. Can't she shut her kid up?" Some will say, "Oh my, I feel so sorry for that parent." Others will say, "Oh my, did that parent hit their child? Let's call the police." Some will walk by without even noticing! Which reaction is right?

The answer is, who cares? *It's none of your business*. Why are you worried about it? Move on. Focus on your own shopping. Pay for it, go home, do the things that are important and live your life.

How does the concept of choice impact on these feelings? Well, if we have the ability to choose how we feel, then should we not be able to choose *how we react and think?*

Imagine your road is paved with the words here. To begin with, you've got serenity, enthusiasm, compassion and appreciation. This continues on through acceptance, self-esteem, admiration and surprise. Reflect here on when you experienced these feelings. Think about where you

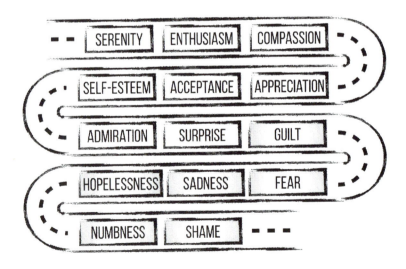

were. Think about why you felt this way. Think about who was involved.

Next, focus on the remaining words: guilt, fear, shame, numbness, hopelessness, and sadness. As the words change, how do the feelings change? We choose how we feel all the time. The feelings that are easier to feel, however, don't feel like a choice. We don't think about or analyse when we're feeling enthusiasm or compassion, because it feels good. We just go with it. When we start to feel guilt or fear, sadness or hopelessness, we start to analyse it and dig deeper, because we don't like feeling that way. With the positive words, there is no victim. However, when it's counterproductive, shaming, or painful, *we become the victim*.

When we feel like the victim, it's because we've chosen to.

The power of choice is a hard concept for some to grasp. It's something that you have always had, that you will always have, and that no one can ever take away from you. We forget, for whatever reason, that we have the power of choice in the first place. Why is that? Is it cultural? Is it societal? Is it our own behaviour? Do we purposely choose to relinquish this control in order to please others? Do we even know that we've done this?

This can all link back to those triggers. Some words feel good because there is no victim, but others can incite the feeling of being victimised.

If we think we've been made to feel guilty, or we are feeling fearful, hopelessness or sadness, perhaps because we're on the receiving end of shitty leadership — or we are now aware that we incite these feelings in others — we can now see how choice plays into our leadership. How does this balance your frequency to remain focused? This is where you turn on your frequency and say, "Trigger! I'm not going to accept you. Instead, I'm going to stay on my road."

To balance your feelings and choices, you have to be conscious. You must listen to your own thoughts. Then you have to become conscious of your own reactions. You must listen and observe yourself. This self-awareness means you'll be able to recognise your own triggers and emotions, and course correct where appropriate.

Whenever you're starting to feel like you're going off frequency, that awareness is the first step towards adjusting. If you know which words or thoughts trigger you, identify them. Then, when they happen, you can refuse to take the bait.

Personally, my truest trigger is when I am blamed for something I didn't do. I live an authentic life, and I take ownership of my errors; if I make a mistake, I own it, and I move on. I recover, I fix it, and I move forward. I don't hold a grudge. I don't have time.

When I get blamed for something I didn't do, I will show kindness the first time — but probably only the first time. If you keep pushing it, be careful, because Mark's going to be out for blood now. I will go to the *nth* degree to prove that I didn't do what you're accusing me of. Being purposefully blamed for something I didn't do is my absolute number one trigger.

But that is my choice. If I succumb to that trigger, I have no one to blame but myself. Being aware of it means I can watch out for it — I can recognise the emotions it incites, I can see the red flags and the language of blame. I can move to course correct, to let go, to distance myself, to not allow that trigger to send me into a spiral.

We make choices all the time and often know that we should be doing better. Things like diet, exercise, sending a text whilst driving — we all know *how* to be better, but sometimes we just don't do it. Why is that?

Our emotions are part of those choices, too. Recognise your triggers, choose different reactions and keep your focus.

OWNERSHIP & MAINTENANCE

Remember, again, that the happy emotions rarely feel like a choice. Many people never recognise that they're choosing to feel the way they do. It just doesn't feel like a choice, because when it feels good, we don't think about it.

When we're talking about owning how you feel, think and react, the key is to realise that when it feels good, *that's also a choice*. If you can recognise that, then when it starts to feel negative, you can see the choice more plainly. You can think about why that's triggering you, and why you are choosing that response. Why are you choosing to potentially feel like a victim?

A prime example of this goes back to the subtitle for our last book. When I ask the question, "Are you a shitty leader?" people either laugh and say, "Oh, you know what, I never thought of it that way. Let me explore it." Or they look at me and say, "Go away." Or, "You're egocentric, I'm not talking to you about this." Some people, when they hear "Are you a shitty leader?" choose to see the humour in it, which was the intention, and then they recognise that it is a behavioural choice and doesn't make you a shitty person.

However, some choose to feel like a victim. Some people reading this right now feel like a victim. But whether you laugh or whether you rage, neither reaction is because of me. Those are choices. If you're not able to recognise that, you won't be able to manage those emotions. You'll feel like a victim, under the control of your feelings.

Those who choose to feel a strong negative reaction to the subtitle of the book, in my experience, are generally feeling that way for a reason. Because you have control over your own actions. You're choosing your thoughts, and these impact on your mood and well-being.

If you constantly choose to feel like shit, then you're going to feel like shit. Eventually, you're going to start making others feel like shit, or incite others to feel like shit in your presence. It's the same with people who are upbeat and positive, who give off a good vibe and energy. You can feel it when they walk in the room! You're happy to be around them because they just give off this vibe of joy.

When is enough, enough? Let's say you worked for the same shitty leader for a couple of years and she is late or cancels your weekly coaching sessions. She rarely gives feedback. When she does, she yells and plays the blame and shame game. She is perceived as unapproachable, and you feel your confidence fading as a result. You have options. You could do nothing different, which means nothing changes. You could come prepared to raise your concerns in your next session and see if it happens again. You could lodge a complaint with **HR**. You could complain to your boss's boss. Or you could send your boss an email in a warm tone to help her understand your concerns.

The bottom line is that doing nothing is also a choice. When you do nothing, you create the perception that you're the victim. That is going to eat away at your frequency, and that can become a trigger in itself.

How you choose to react to a situation is your choice. That outcome is governed by behaviours, which then lead to a feeling, and then to action. Your responsibility is simply to be aware of this. Visualise when that interaction occurs: how do you want to respond? We are not defined by what happens to us. We are defined by how we choose to respond. You have the power to respond without making yourself a victim.

As a side note, there are times when it is entirely appropriate for you to respond as a victim. If you're experiencing abuse, you should respond as a victim would respond: get help. Get out of the situation. Hold the abusing party responsible. You've done nothing wrong if you feel as though you're a victim in that situation — you are.

It's the situations where you're not a victim, but choose to respond as if you are, that we're talking about here.

Maintenance means learning how to indoctrinate this into your everyday life. How will you remember to do this? How will you remain self-aware? How will you be self-aware enough to know you're self-aware?

F TO THE POWER OF THREE

There are three 'F's to focus on here: **Feelings, Focus and Frequency.**

The How of Self-Awareness

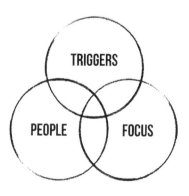

How do you connect feelings and frequency? You can achieve this through becoming more self-aware, through remaining on your road and protecting your frequency, owning your frequency, and managing your frequency. You've become aware of your triggers and you choose to be kind over right, whenever possible and applicable. You've set your boundaries and articulated them effectively.

To remain focused, you must balance your feelings and your frequency, and to do that, you have to remain self-aware. Again, and again and again, we come back to this essential skill: *becoming and remaining self-aware.*

SHITTY LEADERSHIP CHOICES: A REAL-LIFE EXAMPLE

I consulted for a company where I was asked to create and develop a very detailed training strategy. The executive sponsor of the program, who was also head of HR, was somewhat strong-minded and perceived as a bit of a narcissistic leader. She was a blamer and a shamer. It was very hard for her to retain staff at her organisation. She was patronising and condescending and would make rude, sarcastic comments when giving feedback.

During the year and a half that I worked for her, I noticed that she was becoming the main topic of my venting. I was constantly frustrated. How could someone at her level demonstrate those behaviours so freely? How could she do all this, and still think she was leading by example?

I knew it wasn't just my lens and my view. Whenever someone mentioned her name, most people would roll their eyes and make derogatory comments. I made a few attempts at obtaining feedback, but she wanted no part in it. My attempts to manage up and work with her were shot down. Eventually, I chose to give up, and felt Sunday despair for a while. I hated going to work. For a while, a part of me quit-but-stayed — until I came to an important realisation.

I had to make a decision. Because, as it was, I was allowing this person to be my energy vampire. She didn't care about me as an employee, whether or not I worked there, or how I felt about certain things. She wanted no part of it, and made no attempt to fix it. The choice I made then was to 'kill her with kindness,' as they say. I stopped taking the bait. I wasn't going to be condescending and rude and patronising and childish. I actually took a vested interest.

When I saw her, I would say things like, "Oh, hi, how are you? How are things? I heard this, yeah, is everything okay? Oh, a big job." I would make idle small talk, but I did it from a place of sincerity. I tried to make her my best friend, because I wanted to lead by example in the hope that she would see what I was doing.

I wished for too much, as it turns out, because she didn't actually care. Nor did she change. But something changed: me.

My new behaviour actually made me feel better. I stopped venting; I stopped allowing her to be the energy vampire that she didn't care that she was, nor did she probably even intend to be. I stopped expecting her to change, and I took accountability and responsibility. *I changed how I saw it.* Because we're not defined by what happens to us, we're defined by how we choose to handle it. I decided to handle it as a non-shitty leader.

I figured out how I had allowed her to be my trigger. I released the shame and the victim mentality. As soon as I stopped playing the victim, what she said and did no longer mattered. I didn't think about it. I just moved on and accepted that there would be rework. I stopped caring because I found my frequency and stayed on it.

I balanced my feelings with my frequency, which allowed me to focus and choose the path that I needed to walk with this leader, instead of always reacting negatively to her choices.

I stopped blaming her for making me the victim, because *I realised I was actually making myself the victim.* When I realised that, when I found my frequency, it was actually quite easy to stay on it. Because when you take back your power of control and recognise that you had it all along, you don't want to give it up again! When I realised that it was *me* making myself feel that way, and not her, it was actually quite simple to change things.

RECAP

Becoming self-aware means remaining on my frequency. My chosen frequency keeps me on a path of self-worth, knowing that I am enough. I know my leadership brand is that I am people-focused, and I never want to lose sight of that fact. I'm aware of my triggers and I avoid them at all costs. When I'm faced with those situations, I confront them head on and with empathy, because those strategies keep me on my frequency. I know how to stay on my proper frequency road, and I don't let the energy vampires in. Because my energy is my commodity and I'm not willing to give that away freely.

REFLECTIVE QUESTIONS

› What are some good choices you've made recently? Why did you make them?

TEN

The Frequency Leadership Matrix

The following tables show a list of leadership actions, both effective and ineffective. As you read through the list, reflect on times when you have demonstrated these.

You've been exposed to the question, "Are you self-aware enough to know you're self-aware?" throughout the book. Now you can test your ability through honest reflections. Have the courage to recognise that you've demonstrated some of these ineffective behaviours. Remember, it's okay to show vulnerability, as once you realise and own it, you can take back control to remedy it and make real-time choices to choose more effective non-shitty behaviours.

Take some time to review the following diagram. Note the behaviours that you've demonstrated.

Leadership Actions (Effective & Ineffective)
Real-time feedback delivery, leads via exceptions, authentic.
Non-Cookie Cutter leadership, bespoke, listens, coaches.
Maintains integrity and trust, leads via development.
Owns leadership brand in real time, accountable.
Authentically self-aware, owns deviations in real-time.
Challenges development through feedback most of the time.
Acknowledges honest career path of staff, develops.
Varying balance of focus - is it about me or you?.
Perceived uncertainty, unclear, lacks focus, ambiguous.
Some inconsistency with delivery, action, behaviours.
Has outburst and lacks some real-time ownership.
Angry with some rare moments of inspiration, emotional.
Perceived as always outside the brand zone or doesn't care.
Harsh tones, verbally abusive or lacks listening skills.
Inconsistent actions with unclear objectives, confusing.
Unaware of shadows cast, toxic, appears unapproachable.
Manager is micro, doesn't ask, knocks down.
Blames and shames, tactless, lacks decorum, rude, arrogant.

What have your reflections revealed?

Now that you've recognised actions, let's look at a list of feelings and actions/behaviours. The actions that follow can incite a feeling (trigger a frequency via a behavioural change) which leads to different actions (and corresponding feelings).

Take a moment to review the list. This is simply a reference guide. The feelings and actions are interchangeable and completely fluid. It's all about your interpretation; there is no right or wrong.

Feelings	Actions/Behaviours
Tranquility	Well-Being, Peaceful, Calm, Engaged
Enthusiasm	Exhilaration, Eager, Passion
Empathy	Compassion, Kindness, Understanding
Appreciation	Gratitude, Care, Thankful
Admiration	Trust, Cooperation, Respect, Awe
Happiness	Hyper, Joy, Glee, Bliss
Gratification	Curiosity, Amusement, Satisfaction
Commanding	Strength, Courage, Determination
Self-Esteem	Confidence, Empowerment
Approval	Contentment, Safety, Acceptance
Wonder	Confusion, Disbelief, Surprise
Anger	Wrath, Defiance, Boredom
Guilt	Resentment, Remorse, Fault
Fear	Blame, Threat, Hate
Sadness	Depleted, Loss, Burden
Hopelessness	Depressed, Resignation
Numbness	Overwhelmed, Frozen, Emotionless
Shame	Disgrace, Embarrassment, Humiliation

What stands out for you the most?

THE FREQUENCY LEADERSHIP MATRIX

What are some of the common feelings and sounds created by these actions, feelings and words? Have a look at the table for some examples. Remember, again, these are merely interpretations. Feel free to write down some of your own.

When you reflect on your past year, what do you find yourself feeling and hearing most?

How It Feels	How It Sounds
Peaceful Inspirational Clarified Aligned Informed Generous Welcoming Responsive Understanding Pleasurable	"I love working here!" "My boss has my back." "I trust you." "I believe in you." "What do you need?"
Varied Calm Vent-worthy Cautious optimism Watchful Wary Guarded Vigilant Thoughtful Content	"I think I'm okay…" "Sometimes I wonder why I still work here." "I wish he/she was a consistent leader." "It's alright, I manage."

How It Feels	How It Sounds
Isolated Ready to give up Really shitty Full of Sunday despair Remorseful Accepting onus Culpable Frightened Anxious A sense of dread A sense of panic Alarmed Apprehensive Dishonoured Disgraced	"Oh no, not again?" "How does he/she constantly get away with this?" "I'll show them!" "I quit!" "I can't take it anymore!" "I'm done!"

And finally, outcomes. Take a look at the table on the next page. The more effective the leader, the more effective the outcome. The words can be quite powerful when read aloud.

Common Outcomes
Builds connections. Maintains high frequency. Expands comfort zones. Encourages enablement Promotes growth. Supports change. Is consistently positive.
Creates sporadic uncertainty. Stifles or limits creativity. Embeds fear. Inspires caution. Halts energy. Is inconsistent.
Staff 'quit and leave' or 'quit and stay'. Enforces apathy. Breeds harsh venting. Creates an 'us and them' mentality. Erodes trust. Increases unnatural attrition. Impacts on clients/customers. Is consistently negative.

This matrix is simply a guide to help you reflect and continue your awareness of the impacts you can have on your own thoughts and feelings and those of others. Let's see it altogether on the following pages.

Feelings	Actions	How It Feels	How It Sounds	Common Outcomes
Tranquility	Well-Being, Peaceful, Calm, En-gaged			Builds connections. Maintains high frequency. Expands comfort zones. Encourages enablement. Promotes growth. Supports change. Is consistently positive.
Enthusiasm	Exhilaration, Eager, Passion	Peaceful Inspirational Clarified	"I love working here!"	
Empathy	Compassion, Kindness, Understanding	Aligned Informed Generous	"My boss has my back."	
Appreciation	Gratitude, Care, Thankful	Welcoming Responsive Understanding	"I trust you." "I believe in you." "What do you need?"	
Admiration	Trust, Cooperation, Respect, Awe	Pleasurable		
Happiness	Hyper, Joy, Glee, Bliss			

Feelings	Actions	How It Feels	How It Sounds	Common Outcomes
Gratification	Curiosity, Amusement, Satisfaction	Varied		
Commanding	Strength, Courage, Determination	Calm Ventworthy	"I think I'm okay…"	Creates sporadic uncertainty. Stifles or limits creativity. Embeds fear. Inspires caution. Halts energy. Is inconsistent.
Self-Esteem	Confidence, Empowerment	Cautious Optimism Watchful	"Sometimes I wonder why I still work here."	
Approval	Contentment, Safety, Acceptance	Wary Guarded	"I wish he/she was a consistent leader."	
Wonder	Confusion, Disbelief, Surprise	Vigilant Thoughtful	"It's alright, I manage."	
Anger	Wrath, Defiance, Boredom	Content		

Feelings	Actions	How It Feels	How It Sounds	Common Outcomes
Guilt	Resentment, Remorse, Fault	Isolated Ready to give up Really shitty		Staff 'quit and leave' or 'quit and stay'. Enforces apathy. Breeds harsh venting. Creates an 'us and them' mentality. Erodes trust. Increases unnatural attrition. Impacts on clients/customers. Is consistently negative.
Fear	Blame, Threat, Hate	Full of Sunday despair	"Oh no, not again?"	
Sadness	Depleted, Loss, Burden	Remorseful Accepting onus Culpable	"How does he/she constantly get away with this?"	
Hopelessness	Depressed, Resignation	Frightened Anxious	"I'll show them!" "I quit!"	
Numbness	Overwhelmed, Frozen, Emotionless	A sense of dread A sense of panic Alarmed	"I can't take it anymore!" "I'm done!"	
Shame	Disgrace, Embarrassment, Humiliation	Apprehensive Dishonoured Disgrace		

THE FREQUENCY LEADERSHIP MATRIX

THE FREQUENCY MATRIX IN ACTION

The charts on pages 109–111 can be useful in two ways. First of all, if you're practising self-awareness, you'll notice the different feelings that your actions incite in others. Say, for example, that I have incited sadness in someone. I can find that on the chart. I can surmise that they're feeling depleted, lost or burdened, or something along those lines. The thoughts that person is having are aligned with sadness; they are thoughts of something they lost, something that has burdened them, or something that is depleted in them.

That person may now feel isolated, and they may feel like giving up. They might feel ultra-shitty. They might feel culpable. They might be in their fight-or-flight mode. They might feel disgraced, dishonoured, and apprehensive. Some of what they're saying, either publicly or to themselves, sounds like, "*Oh, not again. I'll show them, I quit. I can't take it anymore. How do they always get away with it?*" It's very negative; they feel victimised.

What might the outcomes be? That person might quit, or they might quit and stay. It can enforce apathy. It will breed harsh venting. It will increase unnatural attrition. You can also see what probably caused this: the individual was on the receiving end of inconsistent actions with unclear objectives. They felt confusion.

Sadness can, of course, be caused by a lot of things, but this chart can help you categorise some of the most common connections of thoughts, feelings, frequency and leadership.

You can reverse engineer this and read it the other way, too. If you're a shitty leader who is completely inconsistent with your actions, if you give unclear objectives, or you blame and shame your staff, you can see what's going to happen. You tell someone to draft a PowerPoint, but when they send it to you, you say, "What the hell is this shit? You're useless. Oh my, I should have just done it myself." Well, you're going to cause confusion. That enforces apathy. It increases unnatural attrition. It impacts on the customer, the client. It makes the employee think, '*I'll show them. I'm going to quit. Screw you!*' They feel isolated. They feel alone. They feel anxious. That creates thoughts of resignation, burden, loss, hatred, blame. As a result of that, the individuals find themselves on the sadness frequency. That's how it all links together.

You may be realising that you, in fact, have felt this way many times. You may also be realising that, if you own your leadership brand and maintain integrity and trust, if you give real-time feedback delivery, that's going to build connection. It's going to maintain high frequency. It's going to promote growth.

You're going to hear things like, "I love working here. I trust you. I believe you. You do that really well." You're going to feel peace and you're going to feel inspired and generous. You'll be responsive and understanding. Your frequency will be tranquil yet enthusiastic. Your staff will feel appreciation and empathy. They're going to really like what they're doing, because they'll feel valued, aligned, motivated, and inspired — because they work for an active leader.

This matrix works when you recognise when you've felt this way and have incited others to feel this way. It links at both ends. It connects feelings and frequency with outcomes and actions; everything in between can be subjective. That is the point of the matrix. The fact that you're reading and reviewing it and reflecting is a great start.

RECAP

This chart, like every chapter in this section, is all about moving towards self-awareness. Self-awareness takes you on a journey that involves looking inside yourself. Are you firmly on your road? Are you within your leadership brand? Are you tuned into your best frequency? Or are you clueless, wandering, casting dark and stormy shadows everywhere you turn? The first step towards changing is actually *seeing*: becoming self-aware.

Learn what your triggers are and how you make choices. Recognise triggers from others and from yourself. Learn to recognise your own behaviours and understand why certain triggers incite you to react the way you do. Recognise which words, actions, or people incite your internal victim. Ask yourself why you choose that; adjust accordingly and balance your reactions to maintain focus in real time.

Continue to hold a mirror up and examine yourself. Remember that *you choose how you react*. Remember not to take the bait. Remember to unlearn certain negative habits and choices. And always remember to find, own, and maintain your balance. If you're not there — and none of us are *totally* there — what changes do you need to make?

REFLECTIVE QUESTIONS

› How will you identify your triggers?
› What strategies will you create in order to not accept the emotional connection with an energy vampire?
› How will you identify when you're being your own energy vampire?

ELEVEN

Explanation of Leadership Brand

Your leadership brand is the second pillar of great leadership. It's the second and not the first, because you have to master the first — self-awareness — before you can ever hope to build your authentic brand. You'll never understand who you are until you know who you *were*. So often, when we talk about 'brand,' it feels fake or manufactured — like you have to create it from nothing.

Not so: your leadership brand grows from who you are. When you work on yourself and your authenticity, the best and most talented parts of who you can be as a leader will shine. Once you have the ability to see who you are and to know who you are, creating your brand is easier than you think. You set the boundary of self-honesty. If you're lying to yourself, only you will know.

REVIEWING LEADERSHIP BRAND

Your leadership brand is the second component of active leadership. Up until now, you've become more self-aware; you've explored feelings and actions, behaviours and triggers and awareness of your frequency.

> **Your leadership brand is *how you want to be known, seen and perceived as a leader.***

Do you know how your staff and peers perceive certain behaviours you demonstrate? Have you ever felt misunderstood?

What is your current leadership brand? How do you want to be seen? Have you ever solicited feedback from other people regarding how you're perceived as a leader? How willing are you to travel down this road of discovery? What will happen if you don't like what you find? Can you recognise shitty leadership behaviours in others? How do you know which aspects of your leadership skill set you need to improve on?

As explained in Book One, if you don't have a solid understanding of your own leadership brand, how will others know how to perceive you? Fear can become your brand if you don't take the time to build relationships. If fear were your brand, many people might not want to work with or for you. If you're the type of leader who intimidates, and no one has ever had the courage to provide you with direct feedback, or if no one can trust that you can professionally handle hearing your triggers, odds are, your self-awareness might be quite low in this area.

Most people don't ever think about their leadership brand; they don't know such a thing exists. They have never thought about how they're perceived as a leader. It can be very eye-opening to think about. The natural by-product of that process is that you can't help but become self-aware.

Thinking about our leadership brand just creates that thought process. You can't un-think it once you know about it. This is also commonly referred to as a form of perception management.

The thing is, whether you realise it or not, you already have a leadership brand. Your leadership brand can be shitty, or it can be wonderful, but for you to even understand what it is, you have to take time to think about it — and consider how your brand is changing your workplace and your culture.

When you become aware that your brand exists, you then have to identify what that brand is. If that brand doesn't support who you want to be as a leader, well, now that you know that, you can fix it.

YOUR BRAND MUST BE AUTHENTIC

Your leadership brand doesn't have to necessarily be positive. What it really has to be is *authentic*. The whole concept of the leadership brand is to know who you are, and then to make sure that your brand accurately represents that. When you identify, build, create and then publish your leadership brand with your team, that is your accountability checklist of who and how you want to be seen and perceived. When you match who you are to how you want to be perceived, that builds trust. That's how you show authenticity to your staff.

When you deviate from this, and potentially enter the land of misperceptions off the Ego Continuum, with the risk of being perceived as a shitty leader, you can incite your team to manage up. They'll be prepared to say, "I'm noticing things that are different. What's wrong?" That's a team full of trust and, ultimately, productivity.

This leadership brand isn't something you can manufacture. It's not just you creating it. It's created out of *who you are*. From an authenticity perspective, you're now self-aware enough to say, "Let me start declaring who I am as a leader today, versus how am I perceived."

This is when you've made the connection and know who you are. When you start documenting your brand, if there's a massive disconnection between the behaviours you demonstrate and the perceptions of others, as you're going through the exercise, people are going to call you out on it. You can spot check yourself and correct accordingly.

AUTHENTIC VULNERABILITY

Now that you understand what a leadership brand is, it's time to dive into what this means to you as an individual. That's where we begin, with authentic vulnerability.

This is the next step; the second phase of active leadership. Authentic leadership — authentic vulnerability — is about your behaviour. What you do should identify who you are. These are the core behaviours that you demonstrate.

Personally, I'm a talker. I use humour. I don't mind being cheeky and sarcastic with dry humour. I like to create reflective moments. I like answering questions with questions. I like to incite teachable moments when I can. These are common things for me, and because vulnerability is a strength, I don't mind showing it.

Now is the time to start documenting some of that self-awareness from your leadership perspective. That's the first step in understanding what your leadership brand is. Where does your leadership naturally fall? What behaviours do you naturally tend towards?

After that, it's time to demonstrate a level of genuine humanity and show that you have motivators and needs. Talk openly about the areas where you feel uncomfortable, discuss your known triggers and demonstrate a willingness to let yourself be seen genuinely as you are, and not as you think you should be.

I recently had this conversation with one of the guys at work during his one-on-one. He really struggles with vulnerability. He specifically said, "I'm uncomfortable with that word."

"Could it be," I asked, "because you're a straight, British male?" Our working relationship allows me to be direct and ask questions like this. I wouldn't have said that to just anyone. We share a mutual understanding of a direct approach with humour.

He laughed and said, "Yeah, that probably has a lot to do with it."

I said, "Let me ask you this. What is it about being at work that makes vulnerability uncomfortable?"

"I need to be seen as strong," he said. "I need to be seen as intelligent. I need to be seen as a leader."

I said, "So, when you hear the word 'vulnerable', you think 'weakness'?"

"Yeah, I do."

"Let me ask you this," I said. "When you build up the courage to walk across the bar to chat with that pretty girl, is that not vulnerability? When you ask her out on a second date, when you make your first move, when you buy her flowers, when you tell her that you have feelings for her, when you initiate any kind of romantic intent, is that not also vulnerability? Because there are no guarantees, she's going to say yes."

He said, "I never thought of it that way."

Most people, it seems, don't think of it that way. We create rules, like *"When I'm in the workplace, I should be this, this, this, this and this, because this is who I'm supposed to be."* Where did those rules come from, and why are they there? Why can't you just be who you are, and why isn't that enough? That is authentic vulnerability.

If you're displaying vulnerability, it means you're strong — because you're putting yourself out there and you're taking a risk. You're strong enough to know that if something fails, you're resilient. You won't enjoy the experience, but that's okay. You're going to go on. That's strength.

As Dr Brown reminds us in her TEDTalk of 2010, vulnerability is the courage to put yourself out there. It is that willingness to make the first move to initiate intimacy, to ask someone out, to wait patiently for the doctor to call with your test results. It is a combination of many things. It's taking a risk that we wouldn't normally take, such as giving a lecture, making a public speech or writing a book.

When you put yourself out there, that is a form of vulnerability. When you achieve this, it automatically becomes a strength, because it's something you've conquered.

What people forget is that even if you fail, *you made an attempt*. That should also be commended because you chose to put yourself out there. That is strength. The best thing about displaying vulnerability by letting yourself be exposed, doing something that you're afraid of, or taking any risk, every single time you do it, is that it makes you stronger. Every time you do something with that feeling of vulnerability, you are going to be stronger — because you've survived it. So far, you've survived 100% of your worst days, right?

People so often miss the boat on that, because they get so worked up on the fact that it was a 'failure.' If it didn't turn out the way they wanted, they would go down that shame spiral. They choose to fuel that behaviour and have a warped view of what failure is. They start to feel negative, and then they miss the opportunity. That's when the fear comes in, because vulnerability is supposed to be strength — but because of how most people perceive it, it becomes fear.

If you think of vulnerability as a problem and don't understand how valuable it is, then you're always wearing armour. If you're wearing armour, you can't really make true connections with people, and as a leader, that's what you're supposed to be doing. Leaders are supposed to marshal people towards some vision or output. If they're afraid of vulnerability, how are they supposed to be in front?

RECAP

Your leadership brand is a collection of your star traits as a leader — and part of that brand needs to be authentic vulnerability because otherwise, the whole brand will seem fake. Allow yourself to be seen as you are, and then determine the components of your leadership brand based on who you are. If you fake it, if you don't know who you are, you can't create it. If you create it with who you *think* you are, instead of who you actually are, you're going to be misaligned most likely the misperceptions will continue.

Listen, you could create a leadership brand that's all bullshit. You could create a completely fabricated brand that is absolutely based on who you think you *should* be as a leader. But if there's nothing authentic about it, then when you present it to your team, they're going to see right through it.

If I wrote a leadership brand that was all linear, strict and formal, following all the rules, it wouldn't last. All you'd have to do is hang out with me for 30 seconds to see that it's not me at all. I can't carry that brand as it's not authentic. If someone wants to blow smoke and create something completely fake, that's fine — but it will backfire. You will get called out.

If you're following the book, if you're following the instructions, take the time to reflect on this and get it right. Don't worry — you'll get there. It just takes time. We're building it together.

REFLECTIVE QUESTIONS

› If the concept of showing vulnerability is a fear, ask yourself why.
› If you can expand your comfort zone outside of work, ask yourself why it is difficult to do this inside of work.

TWELVE

Building and Marketing

This is about the practical means of *how* to make a leadership brand. It will include *five key components* to developing your leadership brand, a walk-through of what that looks like practically, and an overview of how critical it is to build trust and communicate these components to your team — giving them permission to call you out when you veer off-course. Managing up!

Review and reflect on the following areas, as of today:
- What is your leadership brand?
- Are you an effective or ineffective leader?

Your leadership brand is how you want to be known, seen and perceived as a leader.

Answer the following:
- Do you know how your staff and peers perceive the certain behaviours you demonstrate?
- Have you ever felt misunderstood as a leader?
- Can you articulate your current leadership brand?
- Have you ever solicited feedback from other people regarding how you're perceived as a leader?
- How willing are you to travel down this road of discovery?
- What will happen if you don't like what you find?
- Do some see you as a shitty leader? If so, why?
- How do you know which aspects of your leadership skill set you need to improve on?
- Do you have the ability to look honestly inside yourself and determine your own ineffective behaviours?
- How do you know you're giving your staff what they need unless you've asked them, or had them provide honest feedback?
- What are the shadows you cast?

In creating your leadership brand, you will be required to reflect and call on your courage to:

1. Demonstrate a level of genuine humanity and acknowledge that you, too, have motivators and needs.
2. Talk openly about areas where you feel uncomfortable, or your known triggers.
3. Be willing to let yourself be seen genuinely as who you are, and not the person you think you should be.

Creating your leadership brand permits you and encourages you to be human; in fact, isn't that really the common thread that binds us all together?

This chapter delves more deeply into the concepts of vulnerability as strength. By the end of this section, you will have completed and built your own leadership brand that you can share with your team. The intent has multiple purposes. You declare who you are as a leader and your staff is now aware. They can help you ensure that you remain on point. When you deviate, they can offer proactive advice on creating an environment where managing up is an accepted practice. This also reduces misperceptions through unknown branding, eliminates confusion and improves communications. This concept helps to create an engaged workforce.

THE FIVE KEY COMPONENTS

The five key components of your leadership brand are:
1. Your personal leadership styles
2. What's important to you?
3. What do you need?
4. Potential misperceptions
5. Your key drivers

Let's break each one of these down.

Your personal leadership styles
This is *who you really are* — your elevator pitch. Are you more people-focused or data-driven? Are you a linear or creative thinker? Are you an introvert or an extrovert? How would you define your style, based on these areas?

If someone asks me, "What kind of leader are you?", I say: "I am a straight-to-the-point, passionate, people-oriented, reformed shitty leader."

It's to the point. It rolls off my tongue because I own it. It's me. When you're truthful with yourself, it's easy to be truthful to others. When you're telling the truth, you don't need a good memory.

What's Important to You?
What do you stand for and believe in? This should come out of your self-awareness. How do you want to be led, and want to lead? How *you* want to be led is based on *your* preferences. How you lead should be based on *how the people you lead want to be led*.

What Do You Need?
This includes your motivators and potential triggers. What do you need to avoid those things from happening?

Personally, I need honesty and truth. I need to be challenged. I need simplicity. I need teamwork and the occasional, "Kudos" or "Good job" from my superiors. All these things will help reduce my triggers. If you're not getting what you need from your people, it might be time to talk about it.

Potential misperceptions
These are common misperceptions about me, which I sometimes feel I need to defend.

For example, I have received feedback on my performance plans in past jobs that I am talkative and long-winded. Now, I do like to talk; there's no greater joy for me than getting paid to speak for 50 minutes because no one can interrupt me. It's fantastic! However, when someone says to me, "God, you talk a lot," I'll respond in one of two ways:

Either, "Yes, I do, you're right — and I've got some really good stuff to say. You should listen."

Or, "Yeah, and I'm going to keep talking if you don't course correct. If you don't stop me, then I'll keep talking and assume that what I'm saying is working for you."

That's how I mitigate my misperceptions: I either own it as part of who I am, or allow others to correct me and do my best to improve. I know I have a few staff members who are very direct and to the point, and don't like long, drawn-out conversations; I'm not going to do long monologues with them because I know that's not what they like. If I do that, they're going to perceive me differently. They might think I am wasting time or being rude. But since this misperception is something I'm aware of, I can work with them to avoid any discomfort wherever possible.

There will always be a few misperceptions. We can't control how others perceive us, but we can effectively communicate and clarify. Some people misperceive directness with rudeness, just like my confidence gets misperceived as conceit or arrogance. The fact that I am passionate makes some people think I'm being emotional — but all I'm doing is expressing emotion. People easily confuse the two. Managing these misperceptions is about being aware. That's the only way to address and avoid the misperceptions of yourself as a leader.

Remember in the Ego Continuum? It's the way I see myself versus the way others see me. If I'm aware of it upfront, I can just control it and own it. That's being a non-shitty leader — because I'm making it about them, and not about me.

Your key drivers

Key drivers are *what I want you to see and feel about the things I value.*

It's how I create comfort for a variety of people. When I make it about them, what does that mean for them? These are the things that are driving you to behave a certain way, so that you can be on point with your leadership brand. How can you make sure your people really get the most out of your leadership?

This doesn't mean you're changing yourself to please people; this doesn't mean you lose authenticity. I'm not asking you to not be yourself; I'm asking you to put other people first. Seek to understand the other person's point of view before you make your own.

What you might find is that if you're following the context of leadership, providing feedback in the way that it is best perceived by the receiver and your intention is to modify a behavioural output for greater performance — then why wouldn't you modify your own?

You're not changing who you are. You're changing your approach to suit them. This is about interacting with others in an organic way. It really does take two to have a relationship, after all.

If I know things are going smoothly, these are the key drivers that are going to get us there. It's not about pleasing other people; it's about serving other people and the vision that everybody's supposed to be working towards.

A WALK-THROUGH OF BUILDING THE BRAND

To get even more specific, let's look at my own personal leadership brand, and how these components play into it. From **my personal leadership style**, I am people-focused.

What's important to me? I strive for effective communications. I have a desire to encourage. I'm accountable. I believe that vulnerability is a strength. I desire change and fun and democracy wherever possible.

What do I need? As a leader, I need honesty and truth. I need to be challenged. I need simplicity. I like the occasional, "Well done" feedback, and I need teamwork.

In terms of **possible misperception**: people sometimes misconstrue my passion. They say, "Why is Mark upset?

Why is Mark frustrated? Why is Mark angry?" Mark isn't any of those. Mark is just passionate.

I have a people-focused creative style, as opposed to linear. I'm not much of a data numbers kind of guy. I believe in data, and I like data, but I don't lead by it. I lead through that people-focus first, then together we focus on the data and issue.

I'm the intuitive guy. I always want to know how people are feeling first, before we move on to complete the task. What's important to me is what drives my values. I want the team I lead to be honest and integral. I want them to challenge me.

What are my **key drivers**? I am motivated and inspired by people who are authentic, through self-awareness where there's no blaming and shaming, where there are teachable moments, mutual respect and we work smarter, not harder.

Other mantras that make up my key drivers: I wear my heart on my sleeve. It doesn't mean I'm emotional. Vulnerability is a strength, not a weakness. I do not shy away from conflict or difficult situations, but I choose to be respectful. I believe and support real-time feedback. If you're not a part of the solution, then you're part of the problem. Don't come to me whining; come to me with solutions and we'll figure the rest out together. If you're the smartest person in the room, you're in the wrong room. You're the average of the five people you spend the most time with. Actions speak louder than words.

This is me.

Imagine if ten new employees started in a new company, with me as their direct leader. On the first day, I have individual one-on-ones where I ask them, "How do you like to be led? How do you like to receive feedback?" At the end of the day, I hand them a paper that has all this information on it and say, "By the way, here's what I'm all about as a leader. Take this home and review it, and let's talk about it tomorrow."

Those new employees now know exactly what they're in for. What's more, hopefully we've established trust right from the start, because I've presented myself vulnerably to them. Now they know that vulnerability isn't just safe here, it's expected.

MARKETING YOUR BRAND

Marketing your brand is how you share it with others. Once your brand is complete, how do you use it? Some of the tips that I recommend are posting it at your desk, using it as your framework in your one-to-ones with your team, sharing it with your direct manager and getting their input on it, and asking others to rate your leadership performance against your brand. Do you do what you say you do?

This is almost like conducting your own mini 360-feedback sessions with your team. It's not about you, and to make sure it's about them, you have to solicit feedback. When your staff manage up and they give you, their leader, constructive feedback, you know that they have built trust in you. If they don't, they're constantly saying, "No, everything's fine. You're great." Trust me, you're not always great.

Marketing this means declaring your brand to your team so that they can then be challenged to hold you accountable for it. If you veer off course, do they feel comfortable saying, "What's going on, are you okay? This is what I'm seeing..."

You're teaching them how to manage up, without telling them that's what they're doing.

People think about marketing as promotion, and in a way, you *are* promoting — because you're trying to get them to really get on board with it, to really understand you, to really take notice. Establish a plan and a system to spread the word about your marketing brand, and get your team on board.

THE LINK BETWEEN AUTHENTIC VULNERABILITY AND YOUR LEADERSHIP BRAND

When you know the five components, how do you link authentic vulnerability to those things? Recognise that you're enough as an effective leader. You're able to authentically give others what they need because you can, you care, and you are worthy of that connection.

Personal leadership style, as we talked about, is who you are; your elevator pitch. The self-awareness and vulnerability link happens when you recognise that you're able to give your team what they need and make it about them.

If we then go back to *what's important to you*, as the second stage: "What do I believe in? What are my personal values? How would I want to be led?" The guidelines for that would be how I want you to perceive me, and what do I do that potentially enables shitty leadership perceptions, or disables them? The self-awareness link is recognising that my inability to create true connections can impede my ability to share what is important to me, which prevents me from learning what is important for you.

The third component we talked about is *what you need*. Those are my motivators, which will then hopefully reduce my triggers. What are the inverse actions of your triggers? The vulnerability or the self-awareness here is that "people who have a strong sense of love and belonging believe they are worthy of it," says Dr Brown. When I choose kind versus right, I maintain this mindset so that I'm giving you what you need.

My potential misperceptions, which are *the things I sometimes feel I have to defend* for their past or current developmental feedback, and my commitment from a vulnerability perspective mean that I won't numb anything. I will experience with you the joy, the gratitude and the happy times so that when we feel disappointed, we can also talk about things like shame, grief and fear. I will maintain this by remaining in my leadership brand zone and empowering you to help me remain accountable. I will own my deviations.

The final piece is your key drivers. *What I want you to see and feel.* What are my outputs? What does being led by me provide? To connect with vulnerability, as a leader I will let myself be seen. I will allow myself to be vulnerable as I am, and not act the way I think I'm supposed to.

I will lead with my whole self, even if at times you're not ready to buy-in. I believe I am enough to be that effective leader, but I also believe that you are enough to be an effective employee. That's how we link self-awareness, authentic vulnerability, and leadership brand.

RECAP

There are five key components to building your leadership brand:

1. Your personal leadership styles
2. What's important to you?
3. What do you need?
4. Potential misperceptions
5. Your key drivers

It is essential, through your own self-awareness and authentic vulnerability, to establish for yourself what these are, and then, through marketing, to connect and share this with your team. Along with your superiors, these are the people most likely to hold you accountable for your leadership brand, so make sure you connect with them and build enough trust that they feel comfortable checking in with you and telling you if you veer off-course.

Synthesizing self-awareness and vulnerability with the different components of developing your leadership brand is the shining star here with the three pillars. For this pillar, vulnerability and self-awareness interact with leadership behaviour to create the second pillar, your leadership brand.

REFLECTIVE QUESTIONS

› Fill out the Leadership Brand worksheet on the next page, reflect on it often to make sure you are acting within your brand.

Leadership Brand

Your Name:

Your Top Five Competencies:

Your Personal Leadership Style:

What's Important to You:

What You Need:

Potential Misperceptions:

Key Drivers:

Your Personal Mantras:

Your Inspirational Quotes:

THIRTEEN

Recap & Creating Your Leadership Brand

We've covered a lot in this section, and this chapter will provide an overview to bring everything you've learned together. Then, after tying in a few key points, I'll lead you through an exercise that will help you walk away knowing exactly how to establish your own leadership brand.

HUMANS ARE NOT ROBOTS

Ever since the Industrial Revolution, corporate leaders have been struggling with the fact that humans are not robots. Leadership has been, more often than not, all about how to milk every last drop out of your human machines. We obsess about process, about eliminating mistakes and defects, and forget that by treating people this way we actually hurt our overall success. Because people *aren't* robots. If you treat them that way, you get attrition, you get high turnover, you get rework costs — you get a disengaged workforce.

Stop looking at your process. Stop looking at the way in which you do things. Look at it from a *people* lens first. Then together, you can fix the process.

RE-EXAMINING THE SHADOWS YOU CAST

If you've taken the time to look at your leadership brand and connected it with self-awareness, then your eyes are even more open to the shadows you're casting.

We wrote earlier in the book about the shadows you cast, and you now have a better understanding of what that means; it is a form of perception management. As you consider your leadership brand, understanding the shadows you cast is absolutely essential.

Wherever you go, you're casting shadows — and those shadows can be positive or negative. It's up to you. We *will* affect our staff. If it's intentional, it can have a good effect; if we don't care, we leave behind scars and broken relations.

Perception management theoretically focuses on how to fix misperceptions that have already been formed. It's damage control and recovery. Shadow awareness is a forward lens on perception management; it's stopping those negative perceptions before they happen by changing your behaviour.

Think of it as a change in direction. Normally, we think of our shadow as being behind us. You can't see where it's falling; you can't see the effect you're having.

But when you lean into your brand, which declares who you are as a leader and all the values that are important to you, you're changing direction. Now the shadow's in front of you instead of behind you. You can clearly see how far your shadow is cast. You can see if you're creating shade, or a blinding eclipse.

An eclipse is the opposite of connecting. It's making them smaller. Instead, they should feel relieved. Your shadow should make them think, "I'm protected. He's got my back."

> **Seeing your shadow allows you to get proactive about managing perceptions.**

This is part of your active leadership journey.

SUMMARY OF THE JOURNEY

As you've probably noticed by now, everything in this journey ties together. If you struggle with vulnerability, for example, you're having problems making connections. That means you might need to spend some time analysing your triggers. Or perhaps you're subconsciously struggling with shame. Shame can be a normal by-product when reflecting on your past shitty behaviours — don't spend too much time self-deprecating. Make peace and learn to use your forward lens through innovative disruption awareness!

This is about you becoming a better version of yourself. It's about you learning to really understand your perception management to gain the benefits of an engaged workforce. The better you are as a leader, the more productive and engaged your workforce will be. Why should you care about that? Because a disengaged workforce costs your company millions of pounds or dollars a year, which you might not even realise you're wasting.

How many organisations in the world aren't tracking their own self-inflicted waste?

Innovative disruption happens when you start with this new lens, and that may feel uncomfortable. That's okay. Learn how to accept what may have been part of your past behaviour, and then work towards fixing it.

Through learning or unlearning things about yourself, through authentic vulnerability, you can tap into potential unknown strengths. Vulnerability itself is, in fact, a strength! With true self-awareness, vulnerability becomes less frightening, and perception management starts to come more naturally, where you remain in control of your thoughts, feelings, actions and reactions, in order to demonstrate effective leadership behaviours.

As you create your leadership brand, understanding your shadows, learning how you're perceived and achieving authentic vulnerability are all key. Then you can really analyse: what *is* your leadership style? How do you want to be seen as a leader? What does working for you mean for your staff? What aspects of your leadership behaviours are you willing to declare upfront to avoid unnecessary misperceptions and help your staff hold you accountable?

This kind of leadership leads to an engaged workforce, and at the end of the day, that means a more profitable bottom line.

So now, let's discover together: How do you want to lead?

Revisit the five main components of developing your leadership brand. Get to know where you are on each one:
1. Declaring your personal leadership style
2. What's important to you
3. What you need
4. Potential misperceptions
5. Your key drivers

FOURTEEN

"Feedback, when given well, should not alienate the receiver of the feedback, but should motivate them to perform better."
— *M.O. Manager, Fortune 500 Company*

Reviewing Effective Feedback Delivery

The key to effective feedback delivery is to make it as unique and specific to the individuals you support. It is not about providing some sort of experience for your team as a whole; it is giving each of them what they need individually, in order to help them to be more successful in their roles. This involves a degree of humility and vulnerability, because in order to know what these individuals need, you have to actually connect with them.

What do you know about your current team members? Are there any outside issues that may impact on their behaviours or performance? How could you find out? Should you care about this? Isn't that getting too personal? Why not ask them and figure it out together?

Effective feedback delivery is to provide specific insights for the individual on their task and behavioural outputs, so that this can be modified to promote a greater performance.

THE MOST MISSED LEADERSHIP QUALITY

A question I like to ask groups is this: "What is the number one leadership quality?" Of course, this is a very subjective question. But in my personal and business opinion, based on many years of talking about leadership with people and other leaders, the number one leadership quality — and the catalyst to everything we've covered so far — is **humility**.

People rarely think of humility in answer to this question, because many don't ever think about what humility actually means. According to Merriam Webster's dictionary, humility is "freedom from pride or arrogance: the quality or state of being humble."

We need to revolutionise the way leaders are trained from the beginning. When we get fresh leaders, we use this opportunity to teach them about humility and help incorporate this into their brand from day one. The first thing I always tell new leaders is, "Welcome to leadership. It's no longer about you." This stops them from learning shitty leadership behaviours from other shitty leaders, because humility can't be faked. You're either humble or you're not. Some people think leaders are born and not made; I don't necessarily agree with that because it is actually possible to go from shitty leadership behaviours to non-shitty leadership behaviours through coaching, support, and self-awareness. You can learn humility, and once you have, it's very hard to unlearn it.

This is connected deeply with self-awareness — true self-awareness involves the ability to reflect. Am I lying to myself? It's like those people who are trying to lose weight, and then they go to for fast food and get a burger, large fries and a diet cola. And because of the diet drink, they think they're going to lose weight. They're lying to themselves! I know all about that — because I used to do the same thing to myself all the time. This high calorie fried food won't hurt me, because I'm drinking a diet drink. Ha! That's a good one. (And now I want a burger…) and one I have used many times in the past.

Once you can reflect and recognise that, you can get to that level of authentic vulnerability. You stop lying to yourself. You may recognise your chosen victim mentality. When you get to that stage, you'll see that humility is actually about confidence — because humility means showing vulnerability. It's openly telling your employee, "You're better at this stuff than I am, which is why I'm delegating it to you." If you can say that with true sincerity, that's humility. That's effective leadership.

When it comes to effective feedback delivery, humility is essential. If self-awareness is the inspiration and leadership brand is the initiation, then effective feedback delivery is the catalyst to drive the change.

DELIVERY IS FOR THEM, NOT YOU

Delivery is for them, not for you. If the goal of delivery is to improve an individual's behaviour, then it makes absolutely no sense to deliver feedback to a group. If the purpose of delivery is to help a particular employee develop, then your feedback needs to be catered to that particular employee. Feedback isn't there so that you can apply pressure to your team; it's there for your individual employees to gain the specific insights they need to improve.

When you treat someone with humanity, you receive a humane response. Effective communications promote non-shitty leadership behaviours. If you think back to the first chapter, or reflect back on Book One, we talk about the concept of cookie cutter leadership, where you lead everybody the same.

These cookie cutters will make all of your cookies the same size, but we want people who come in all different shapes and sizes, with all different kinds of needs. That's what makes strong teams. Then it's up to you, as the leader, to find out what those needs are, and provide the feedback accordingly.

Effective feedback delivery covers not only the *what* of your employee's performance, but the *how*. In any performance management system, I have found that many companies focus solely on the *what*, from an objective perspective.

If I were to use an example of a typical performance objective, we might say that our goal is for Employee X to reduce executive escalations by 50% by a certain date. That's the *what*.

The *how* refers to the actions and behaviours Employee X demonstrates to get there. The what is the metric; it focuses on the end result. What it doesn't focus on are the behaviours demonstrated, which incites actions and feelings in others. If I hit my goal of reducing executive escalations by 50%, but I was a corporate bully and a complete toxic mess to work with; rude, belligerent, a poor communicator — well, then I left puddles of toxicity in every stretch of my path towards my goal. I alienated myself from three departments. I made people cry when they left. I incited people who felt Sunday despair and not want to come to work.

None of this was in my documentation, because it's not part of the *what*, it's the *how*. If I'm going to be rated on my objectives solely on the what and I hit my number, but I've pissed off or upset 40 people in the process, then how does that make me a superstar? Unless you're looking at the *what* and the *how* together, you're missing 50% of the potential problem — which contributes to shitty leadership.

Effective feedback delivery addresses the *what*, of course; those goals are important. But it also addresses the *how*, because if one person is hitting their goals while decimating the rest of the workforce, then overall, they're hurting your company.

RECAP

When you accept a leadership role, you need to understand what it means authentically. If your focus is skewed and you continue to engage in behaviours that are perceived as making it all about you, you will be ineffective. No changes will occur. Demonstrating a level of care and compassion is how you can adjust to the needs of your staff. The perception that you boss people around won't gain you leadership points. You're likely to be perceived as egocentric, mean or simply not very effective.

Remember, we manage process and we lead people. When we manage people, it becomes invasive. Most people prefer not to feel controlled. As leaders, how do we lead those people? How do we lead those who don't particularly like to feel managed?

Effective feedback delivery is solely about making the process about them. The purpose of constructive feedback in any leadership role is to *provide specific insights for the individual on their tasks and behavioural outputs, so that this can be modified to promote a greater performance*. It is not about being right. It is about setting them up to succeed.

FIFTEEN

Why Delivery Matters

I'll say it again! Great feedback delivery is not about you — it's about them. Excellent feedback delivery will take everything you've learned up to this point and apply it to those two questions. Great feedback has a purpose — but how do you and your staff define 'great'?

Great feedback is delivered effectively to the receiver, regardless of whether it's constructive or positive.

If your goal is to truly meet the needs of your staff, to help the receiver become more effective at their job, then you won't care whether you're proving yourself right — you'll be kind enough to deliver this feedback in a way that is actually received and implemented. That involves trust on both sides.

INCORPORATING THE TWO QUESTIONS

Inspiring your staff as a leader doesn't come from cute posters with clichéd quotes on cubicle walls. Active leadership, when properly executed, *creates* inspirational moments. It's those moments that you remember for a lifetime.

Focus on approaching leadership from a non-cookie cutter perspective. When you shove beautifully individual bites of cookie dough into a mould, you turn out identical cookies. That's beautiful — but it's not inspiring. It is the opposite of effective leadership, the opposite of active leadership, and the opposite of how feedback should be delivered.

In well-executed active leadership, there's nothing cookie cutter about it. Of course, there are some fundamentals of leadership that are the same across the board, but the approach you take with each person must be unique because you're talking about different people.

Effective feedback delivery is engaging with your team through your self-awareness and leadership brand. You are aware of the two questions, and you ask those two questions. This sets the stage and tone for your future feedback delivery sessions.

You know the two questions already, but this chapter is about being able to instil your newfound skills into that questioning process. Using what you've now learned, ask yourself the questions from a fresh perspective.

› How do you like to be led?
› How do you like to receive feedback?

If you ask those questions with an open mind, from your own sincerity and humility lens, remembering all you've learned up until this point, you can then simply take your team's responses on board and give them what they need.

You listen, take notes and provide what they have asked for. You've asked them questions you wanted an answer to. They answered, now give them what they need. This should all be about simplicity.

> **Ask them how they like to be led. Ask them how they like to receive feedback. Take notes. And then, do it.**

This is where you get to show your staff what you're made of. This is the catalyst to drive change. It's you declaring that you are trying to improve. Don't be afraid to let your staff know that you are working to develop your own leadership abilities. That is also a great way to demonstrate humility. *I'm trying to become a better leader, to best lead you. I'm learning, because the way I was doing it before wasn't really working, was it?*

If you've had a shitty boss for years, and then one day your boss says to you, "You know what? I haven't really been optimised in my leadership ability, so I'm learning some new ways and I'm making an effort to improve," who's not going to respond well to that?

Show them that you mean business, and that this humility and effort is going to continue for the long haul. Treat individuals as individuals. Learn how to deliver feedback specifically based on the receiver. Being an inspiring leader starts with getting to know your staff.

FEEDBACK IS NOT AN F-WORD

If you're like most employees and managers who hate the word "feedback," you dislike the term because of the expectation it imposes and how it generally feels for both parties.

When you approach most people in the workplace and say, "Do you have a minute? I'd like to provide you with some feedback," 90% of the time their reaction is, "What did I do wrong?" Part of fixing the global epidemic in shitty leadership is also changing the skewed perception that people have of the word "feedback." Feedback should not be feared. Feedback should be fun and engaging. Feedback should be inspiring.

Constantly facing toxicity in any environment, but especially our work environment, can start to affect our health. When feedback delivery is not engaged to benefit the receiver, that ship has sailed, the boat has sunk; you've lost the opportunity to positively influence them in any way, shape, or form during that moment. This constant toxicity continues to perpetuate disengaged cultures — rework increases, apathy ensues, and people don't enjoy coming to work. They quit and stay and that just continues the cycle, which feeds the global epidemic.

EFFECTIVE FEEDBACK DELIVERY IS CONSTRUCTIVE

If you want your feedback to be constructive, because you're trying to alter performance or modify behaviour, what messaging is required? What are they doing wrong? What are they doing that they shouldn't be doing? Do they know they're doing it wrong? How are you going to approach it?

You have to take a little bit of planning time to think about the best approach here. If the employee is straight-talking, they don't generally make mistakes and they've declared how they like to receive feedback, then providing it should be relatively simple. Only the exceptions cause concern.

Exceptions are the challenging employees that can be argumentative or choose not to take constructive feedback well — those are the ones that I would have deeper conversations with.

Before I engage in the feedback, I would say, "How do you like to receive feedback?"

But this type of employee probably wouldn't respond well, even to that. "I don't care. Just do your job and shut up. This is pointless."

In this instance, you just have to keep asking questions: "Listen. Do you know why I'm asking these questions?"

"I don't care."

"What if you chose to care, just for two minutes? Can I ask you to do that?"

"No. I'll give you 30 seconds."

My 30-second spiel is this, "Part of my job as a leader is to provide feedback. Part of your job as an employee is to receive feedback. We need to find a way to meet in the middle. I'm happy to provide you with feedback in any way you would like to hear it. This is not really something we can avoid, but we can make it the best it can be, based on the fact that we're working together. I could just deliver it in a way that makes it about me, but I would much rather deliver it in a way that's about you and takes your preferences into account."

Most people, when you lay it out like that, will say, "You know what? Okay." They will see the intention. They will see that you're trying to make an effort. 80-90% of the time, it will be successful, because people will just appreciate the fact that you care enough to talk about it in this way.

Remember, the number one leadership strength behaviour is *humility*.

> **If everything you do comes from a place of humility coupled with kindness, along with a bespoke approach, it can't really go wrong, can it?**

The purpose of constructive feedback is for the receiver to recognise that a behavioural change is required in order to improve an outcome. This needs to have positive elements associated, but it so rarely does. When you're constantly in the cycle of being told what you're doing wrong, you start thinking, "Why the hell am I here? Because it seems like I can never do anything right."

If you give only negative feedback, based purely on what you've seen through your own lens, you're not really delivering it in the way that will improve the outcome. This approach also contributes to shitty leadership perceptions in the form of corporate bullying.

TWO SCHOOLS OF FEEDBACK

Cookie cutter leadership avoidance means not assuming that every person reporting to me is the same. Then again, there will always be trends and consistencies, and in the varied world of feedback, most styles fall into one of two different overall styles. There are people who like very direct feedback; they don't like the sugary, syrupy sweet stuff. They just want you to tell them what they need to improve. Your feedback might sound like this: "You messed up. You did this. Don't do it again."

Generally speaking, when you meet with them to discuss it, these people already know you're going to talk about it.

They will probably bring it up first, and they might already have come up with a solution. They don't need nurturing. They don't want the hug. They don't need the validation. They just want you to leave them alone. It's not that they don't like feedback; they just prefer things to be done in a direct, business-like manner.

The second group, as you might be able to guess, is the exact opposite. This is the crowd that will thrive with a little bit more support and understanding. They are generally the people who avoid confrontation and see feedback as confrontational. When you draw that out of them, and you help them to understand that feedback is a positive, not a negative — that it's not about catching them doing things wrong, but about catching them doing things right — you can help them respond well to feedback. They'll prosper with more connection through this process, with some reassurance that you're on their side and a healthy portion of positive reinforcement.

Regardless of the approach, the outcome should be the same — you should have a satisfied employee who has heard feedback in the way that works for them.

That is the goal, and however you need to approach the process to successfully get to the goal doesn't really matter. That's the key to active leadership. It also reinforces that you're not making it about you. You're making it about them. That is the mark of a non-shitty leader.

That is the biggest message in all of this. You are figuring out a way to deliver the feedback so that it alters performance for a greater outcome, and you're making it about *them*. What do they need to be successful? And remember, success is defined however they want it to be defined. If someone just wants to come in every day, do their job consistently, and stay where they're at — and that's successful to them? Great! That's fine with me. Not everyone wants to go after my job. Not everybody wants to be an entrepreneur or the president of the company. As a leader, you can't reflect your career aspirations onto your staff and think that they're wrong if they don't want what you want. Your feedback is for *them*.

How can their idea of success and the needs of the company meet? Feedback will help both of you discover that. If you find something they love doing, you'll know where to assign it. If there's something they're struggling with, your feedback can either reorient them or help them improve. But for any of that to be successful, you have to make that feedback about *them*.

BAD FEEDBACK IN ACTION

Sometimes the worst feedback is no feedback at all; it's those silent communications.

I was consulting at this company for a while, and they had experienced lots of change and large turnover. One day, I got a new boss who was a senior consultant with a similar background to mine! We had more in common than not — but we didn't always see eye-to-eye. The things we didn't have in common were, at times, a bit contentious.

At one point, the company was going through a major shift, and I created an engagement plan to help us through the problem. I shared it with my new boss, and she loved it. I was excited that we were connecting on something!

But then, once the plan was announced, people assumed it was her work — and she didn't correct them. "Great job!" they'd tell her, and even though I was standing right there, she'd simply nod and thank them. No reference to me whatsoever. I brought this up with her, and she basically told me to "suck it up."

This told me that she didn't value my performance. She didn't care. The nonverbal feedback right there was, "You're not worth anything to me. In fact, I'm using you. I'm exploiting you. There's nothing you can really do to succeed here because if you do anything well, I'm going to take credit. And if you do anything bad, I'm not taking any responsibility for it. I'm throwing you under the bus, buddy."

That's truly the worst kind of feedback.

Bad feedback can also come in misguided pushes — when you feel like you have to say something, anything, even if there's nothing your employee's doing wrong. There's this strange idea that all reviews must contain a negative, but what's the point of that?

A friend of mine was working at a company with a very distant supervisor who didn't really give any feedback to anyone until their annual review. That, right away, shows she's not delivering feedback in real time; no one would have any idea if they were doing a good job or not! Employees would approach her, asking for feedback, asking if there was any way they could improve, and she would shrug them off. She had checked out.

Well, when the yearly reviews came out, my friend got a lot of great marks. Then, at the end of the session, she asked if there was any way she could improve. The only feedback this supervisor could provide?

"You should change the way you do your makeup."

She claimed her makeup was a problem, that it was distracting. What she realised, she told me, was this: "She couldn't think of anything bad to say, but she had this idea that a review is where she'd find something wrong — not necessarily where she'd find something right."

This supervisor missed a serious opportunity.

> **Instead of supporting her employee, she nit-picked in a truly unproductive way.**

If you're trying to search for something bad to say, just stop. What's the point? Feedback should be beneficial for the receiver, and picking something to criticise at random is not beneficial.

Another classic example of bad feedback is the one based on emotion. I was sitting around a boardroom table once, at an all-employee meeting. A senior executive asked about a customer complaint, and the answer provided was one he didn't like. He immediately yelled at the employee, in front of about 30% of the entire company: "You're incompetent, you need to find more information, and don't waste my time!" Can you imagine how the employee felt? The emotional outburst was in no way productive or helpful — in fact, it almost lost the company a valuable employee. Emotional feedback might make you feel better, but that's not going to help your team.

LEADERSHIP INTEGRITY

Leadership integrity is not about *finding* the feedback; it's not about looking for something to nit-pick. It's about delivering the feedback in real time based on an employee's needs and goals for behavioural outcomes.

Aside from the two overall styles of feedback: a direct or a softer approach, there are also two types of feedback delivery: ad hoc and developmental. Ad hoc is in real time. The developmental stuff is the stuff that can wait for your next one-on-one. It's not time-sensitive. During the developmental meetings, however, you can reference the ad hoc feedback and note how it was received. "Here's some ad hoc feedback we discussed in the last few weeks. I've noticed an improvement already, which is great. Keep doing more of that."

Developmental one-on-ones will also help me understand where you want to be six months from now, or even 12 months from now. Where do you aspire to be career-wise, and what can we do, developmentally, to help you get there?

Leadership integrity is about helping them improve, but not trying to 'get' them. If you want to reroute trust, try and hide a 'lesson' in your constructive feedback. If you want to retain trust, have an adult conversation about that lesson instead of hiding it and ask for their input.

When you use sarcasm, when you're patronising, when you use condescension or when you play games, you're making it about you. You're not making it about them. Odds are, you're trying to be right, not kind.

Your leadership brand comes into play a lot here, because your leadership style and the culture you work in will define what's appropriate and what's not. Say you're singing in a choir, and you hit the wrong note. Suddenly, the director stops and says, "Good job with that wrong note, buddy!" Now, how they receive that totally depends on the choir. In many situations, that's a terrible delivery that will do nothing but embarrass and alienate the singer. It's terrible leadership.

Then again, if the choir has a close-knit relationship, if they use a lot of humour and there are fun pot-shots taken back and forth all the time, then that might be more accepted — it's not meant to be blaming and shaming, and everyone knows it. As long as you know your team and you know the language you speak, you'll know how to deliver each person's feedback. But you have to get to know them.

And, again, ask them how they like to receive feedback. Even in a humour-based environment, there may be people who simply don't want to receive feedback that way. Make sure you're attending to that!

RIGHT VS KIND

Remember, in any situation of conflict or confrontation, you're constantly faced with the choice of being right or being kind. That being said, being kind doesn't necessarily mean you're wrong. It just means you value acting in kindness more than you do demolishing the other side's argument. If that sounds difficult to you, ask yourself: why is it that you want to be right? Do you want the other person to be wrong? Is that really necessary, or kind?

This comes back to self-awareness; recognising what frequency you're on, realising your personal feelings about the employee or the person you're giving the feedback to, and forcing yourself to make it about them. At the end of the day, what you think, personally, doesn't matter.

If you're focused on the individual, at the intersection of what's good for them and the company, then your heart will always be in the right place. You can provide kindness, and you can do it for the right reasons. The purpose of feedback is not to be right: the purpose should always be for everyone to win.

Great feedback delivery, when done in kindness rather than a determined focus on being right, can turn a win-lose situation into a win-win.

I've said it before and I'll say it many times over: nobody ever comes to work to do a bad job on purpose. Even those people who quit but stay. They might not go that extra mile, but they're not going to come to work to purposely do a bad job. They might not care, but they'll do what they're supposed to do to get by. It might not necessarily be a lot, or enough, but they'll get by.

If no one comes to do a bad job, then you can safely assume your team, in the end, *wants* to do a good job. Feedback is supposed to motivate and inspire. You can't motivate anyone until you find out what their intrinsic and extrinsic values are, and then stimulate those so that they self-motivate. You can't motivate anybody to do something. You have to motivate them to motivate themselves.

WHEN YOU FACE SHITTY FEEDBACK

If you find yourself on the receiving end of shitty feedback, there's only so much you can do. Depending upon the level of shittiness that your leader demonstrates, you have a few options. You can do nothing. That is an option. Doing nothing is still a choice as mentioned previously, because sometimes you have to choose your battles wisely. If you've made several attempts and it's not getting anywhere, then you sometimes have to make the call to say, "I'm better than this, and I'm just going to bide my time."

You also have the option of attempting to manage up. I once had a supervisor who gave feedback in the absolute worst way — in the middle of conferences, in front of the team; he'd mock me and everything I was saying. "I'm going to stop you right there," he'd say, "because it's obvious you don't know what you're talking about."

I made attempts to talk to him. I made attempts to say, "Can we start over? Can we level set? Because I find that this isn't working for me, and here's why…" I would explain myself from that perspective. I would tell him what I needed.

Unfortunately, he just thought I was being inappropriate. He thought I was telling him how to do his job. He wanted no part of that feedback. He wanted no part of hearing what I had to say, or what I needed, because upon reflection I now realise, vulnerability was extremely rare and difficult for him. I told him it was affecting my health, that I would need to look for other jobs if things didn't change, and he took that as me threatening him — when I was just trying to tell him where I was at. He wasn't hearing me. But I did try to manage up. In other situations, that can be really effective.

Depending upon the culture, you might have other avenues. You might have HR. You might have a union rep if you're a unionised environment. You might have a good relationship with that person's leader, so you could go a step above them. My recommendation, though, if you're going to go a step above, is to let them know you're doing it. That's scary, of course, because shitty leaders will be prone to retaliate. But it will be worse if you put them on the spot.

Even with something as small as asking for a raise, I always advise giving a signpost to your leader.

Don't put your boss on the spot, especially if you've already got a tumultuous relationship.

If you're going to ask for a raise, let them know in a private, in-person conversation, "By the way, I just wanted to let you know, the next time we meet, I'm going to raise the subject about my compensation. Is that okay?" That way you're signposting, you're not putting them on the spot; you're letting them know that in the coming weeks you're going to talk about it again.

You can do the same with feedback. Say, "Listen. I just want to let you know, I have made so many attempts at improving our relationship, but it doesn't seem to be working. I'm going to ask you one final time if there's an opportunity for us to work through some of these issues together, so that we can make this a more productive working relationship. If not, I'm going to look at exploring other options. It might be that I don't work here anymore, or that I go to others for support. Those aren't threats; I'm just trying to signpost to you so that you don't think I'm throwing you under the bus. I'm making attempts to talk to you, but it doesn't seem to be working, so either help me understand what I'm doing wrong, so I can do it differently, or please know that I will go and seek support elsewhere." That way you're calling it out. You're being vulnerable. You're saying, "I've come to you for solutions and answers and I've made suggestions, but this hasn't worked, so I'm letting you know that if we can't resolve this, I will seek resolution elsewhere."

GIVING THE RIGHT KIND OF FEEDBACK

Now, if you're the leader giving feedback, if it ever gets to the point where you have an employee who has to have that conversation with you, things are pretty dire. Whatever you think you're doing, stop immediately and figure it out.

If you've created an environment where people feel comfortable, you can always try the stop/start/continue exercise. That's where, during feedback, you tell them one thing you want them to *stop* doing, one you would like them to *start* doing, and one you want them to *continue* doing, and then, in a one-on-one, safe environment, you ask them to give the same feedback to you. Now you're soliciting open feedback from your staff.

What I have found is that when your team feels comfortable to give you a 'stop doing,' they most likely have a good level of trust with you. That clues you in that you're giving the right kind of feedback and they feel safe.

If you're getting one-word answers, if they're not truly engaged, if their body language is closed — there's less trust. It's hard to fake it. If you're asking the right questions, you will see a change in productivity. You will see a change in behaviour. You will find you have less constructive feedback to give. There are fewer errors. There is less rework, fewer mistakes, and fewer behavioural outputs that are unnecessary noise and drama. If you're getting it right, you should be able to tell.

Sometimes, though, you can get duped, and they won't tell you to your face how they really feel, because they're just not wired to do that. There is only so much you can do. You're going to run into people like that as well as certain industries where people are less open. They just want to get to work and do their job. Everyone has a sweet spot. You just have to find it. You have to take a leap of faith in recognising when someone else is truly uncomfortable with being vulnerable at work with his or her employer.

Everyone is human, and as we've talked about before, everyone longs for connection. The people that don't think they do are the ones that generally need it the most — and have the hardest time finding it.

TRUSTING YOUR TEAM

A key component of excellent feedback is trust — and not just building up their trust in you. You've got to trust *them*.

For example, some people don't like public displays of gratitude. They don't like to be thanked publicly amongst their peers — it makes them feel uncomfortable. When they tell me that, I don't thank them publicly. If I do things to my employees that they've asked me not to do, even if it's a positive thing like giving excellent feedback, I'm going to erode the trust. I'm going to hear; "I told you I don't like it when you thank me publicly, so why are you thanking me publicly? I'm not being a victim, I'm not pretending I don't want you to when I really do — we're past all that elementary school and playground nonsense."

An adult has told me not to thank them publicly, so I'm not going to thank them publicly. I'm going to trust that they mean what they say. I'm going to keep my feedback — be it positive or constructive — to one-on-on meetings.

I'm going to trust them to tell me the truth, and to correct me if I make a mistake. I'm going to trust that they want to do a good job — feedback is for them, remember? So, if something's going wrong, and I trust that they actually want to fix it, then the issue isn't teaching them a lesson — it's figuring out, together, how to help them improve.

If you've ever worked at a call centre, you'll know that the schedule is very specific and important. At call centres, your attendance impacts on the people around you as well as your customers, which is why you're scheduled for such specific times. If you're due to start at 9:00 AM, you're supposed to be ready to take calls and be on the phone at 9:00 AM or even 8:59 AM.

At a call centre I was supervising, someone was having a habitual problem with lateness, and as it was a militant environment, I had no choice but to document it. If you were a minute late, based on the phone stats, you were considered late. You were put on a performance improvement plan and there was the potential for dismissal. This particular employee was fantastic in every other sense. She was a great employee, but she just couldn't get to work on time, so we were constantly having the same conversations.

If you recognise the definition of insanity, it's repeating the same behaviour and expecting a different outcome. So finally, when we were getting close to a written warning, I said, "Listen, what do we need to do? Because this isn't working. We've talked about this a lot already; this attendance issue downplays all the other great things you do."

I trusted that she wanted to do the best job possible and I worked with her to figure out a solution. As it turned out, there were traffic and childcare issues. I talked to her about scheduling and planning, and was able to alter her schedule so that she could start half an hour later. We were able to make exceptions for people when there was a valid reason to do so, and by making this change, the problem went away.

I trusted her. I acknowledged the good things she did. Then I tried to work out a plan that would work in real life, not just establish goals that she couldn't meet. If you collaborate with your employees to figure out solutions, or you task them with coming up with their own, then you don't actually have to get their buy-in because they've developed it themselves. You trust them, and they become more invested.

RECAP

Some people need feedback that's direct and to-the-point, with zero fluff. Some need more support and positive affirmation. But regardless of how anyone receives feedback, the truth is that almost no one comes to work intending to purposefully do a bad job. If you know that, you know that your team wants to do a good job.

If you can operate from that perspective, you can actually work with them to solve problems and improve — rather than just enforcing irrelevant 'lessons' that will make them feel disengaged with you and with their work. Feedback is vital in a team setting, and they should be able to give you feedback as well. You should be able to trust them, and they should be able to trust you. Excellent feedback can help build that trust.

SIXTEEN

Dictatorship vs Democracy

Sometimes, as a leader, there are times when you have to be a dictator; you just have to tell everyone what to do. There are also times when you can be democratic and let the team lead. Both have pros and cons. They are appropriate at different times and work differently for different leadership styles. Overall, democracy is going to create the healthiest team environment, but sometimes this isn't viable. The key is communicating with your team and explaining when and why you have to do either.

DICTATORSHIPS

Sometimes we have to be a bit firmer than we naturally are. I don't avoid or have any sort of issue with being a strong vocal leader. From my leadership brand, I am naturally a democratic leader, so if I was unbranded, my team would perceive me as being confrontational. I am also not opposed to confronting an issue when it's appropriate to do so however, many hear the word and assume it's a negative. You can confront an issue directly without having to be angry or rude. When I can obtain input from staff to help make decisions, they are more invested, and there is less buy-in work to do.

Now, because it's outside of my leadership brand and not my natural state, when I start saying, "I just need you to do it. Here's why…" I'm perceived as a dictator. That's okay. Sometimes I **have** to be a dictator. Sometimes at work, we get directives that we don't personally agree with. That's fine, but the work still needs to be done. With my own boss, I'm not a yes-man, and I state that on day one. If you're looking for someone to come in and agree with you all the time, then I'm not the person for the job. If you want to be challenged, because I think there's a different outcome or a different way we can do something, then I'm going to give that feedback. But, for those times that it's necessary, if my boss simply tells me, "I don't need your feedback. Just get it done, and do it this way," I'll do it. You don't have to tell me twice.

It's not about me wanting to be right, or do things my way. It's about what's best for the business. I'm going to challenge what's best for the development of the employee, and I'm going to challenge what's best for the customer. If I don't think we're doing something that falls in line with one of those things, then I'm going to question anyone on why we're doing it. That's just who I am, and that's part of my leadership brand. It doesn't mean I think my way is better, and it doesn't mean I just want to challenge you because I want you to be wrong, and I want to be right.

Some people perceive the act of challenging as a negative, but it just means taking a second look at how we're thinking about something. It doesn't mean that I automatically think you're wrong. I might just be wondering why you came to that decision. In some instances, I'm given directives by my clients or my boss that basically sound like, "Mark. Just shut up and go and do it." When I hear that, I just do it, but then I tell my team, "Guys. Here's what we're doing. Here's why. This is a directive from above. We just need to get it done. Let's just move forward."

> **It is still dictating, but it's done through democracy, so that there's no misalignment or misunderstanding.**

The moral of the story is that when you have to be a dictator, explain why, because dictators can be perceived as contributing to toxic environments. A constant dictatorship creates minions. It kills and stifles creativity. It embeds toxicity and creates fear. It doesn't create a culture of feedback, development and growth. It does the inverse. If you want to be deemed as a shitty leader, keep focusing on your inner dictator, and see what happens. Perhaps this has already led to some of your current cultural issues or misperceptions?

DEMOCRACIES

Most of the time, it's best to lead through democracy. Even when you're giving a directive, which could be dictator-like, you don't have to lead through dictatorship. Even if your team wants a dictator, which some people do. Some people prefer to be told what to do. They don't want to strategise with you. In a democracy, you give them what they need. For example, if I'm on a team and there are a couple of things we need to strategise, I say, "I'm going to spend the next half hour brainstorming ideas and being creative on this, this, and this. If anyone does not want to participate in that, I've got this and this for you. If you want to go and get a start on that, I'll call you back in when we've finished brainstorming." If people don't want to contribute, why would you make them?

It's all about giving your staff what they need. Be democratic, even when they want dictatorship.

NEGOTIATING DICTATORSHIP VS DEMOCRACY

Of course, the more common problem is not that people want a dictator — it's that they really, really don't like it when you pull that card. They want to continue to put their two cents in, even though it's not really appropriate. That's when you move to one-on-one specific feedback and tell them, "You know, I can hear that you're struggling with the task that we all need to do. But we all need to do it, so the outcome is not going to change. Do you need to vent for five, ten minutes? Are you frustrated? Is there a problem? Help me understand the real issue behind why you're struggling with this, because at the end of the day, we all just need to do it."

Knowing when to do this, knowing when to rely on democracy or to switch to dictatorship, and knowing how your team's responding — all of that goes back to self-awareness. You have to be aware of your leadership, your team, and the shadows you're casting.

By this time, people should know who I am as a leader. I should know my staff exceptionally well. We should have established the one-on-ones. We should have established relationships, in that my staff is familiar with my leadership style and brand — and I am familiar with them. If I hear or sense hesitation when they've been given a task, I'll say, "Okay, so here are the options. I've shared in the public team meeting that we all just need to do it. This is your part. You haven't done it yet because you're struggling with the directive. I've explained where the directive came from, so I need to understand. Do you want to vent? Is there something else you want to talk about? Because if we have to talk about this a second time, then it's going to become a performance issue, and I don't want that to be the case for you."

Sometimes they just don't understand, or they haven't heard, or they don't know why they're hesitating, but you can't flog a dead horse. Once you say, "It's great that you are so passionate about this, but I need you to do this. Can you do it?" Either they will say yes, realise their own issue and move on, or they won't. Maybe they'll get it off their chest privately, because they've now felt comfortable enough to vent. Maybe they'll suck it up like an adult and just do it, but if not, I reassign the work to someone else and I ding them for a performance issue. It's their call.

If they're not accepting the directive, at the end of the day, it becomes a performance issue for them. As long as I've signposted and explained myself, and they know my leadership brand and that I'm not normally like this, but that the directive has come from above and just needs to be done, then a team member shouldn't have an issue following through with it.

RECAP

At this point, you should be able to readily recognise which leadership style you need to use. You should recognise the members of your team that are having issues. On the Ego Continuum, depending on where you identify your leadership and your balance point, that is what you share within your brand. If I am somewhere in the middle of dictator versus democracy, but I prefer to lead a democratic society, most people will know that, because it's easy to see.

If you fall out of your brand, people will be able to tell. The catalyst for this is whether you've identified who you are authentically. If people know where you are in your brand, do they know that, on the Ego Continuum side, you're more democracy than dictator? Then, they'll recognise it when you're doing something different. And if you signpost and communicate effectively, then you're sharing what they're seeing. You're telling them, proactively, why you're doing something different.

Normally, I'll ask questions and we'll vote. In the rare instance where I'm being dictator-like, people will respond differently. Some will see a dictator as possessing strength, courage, and determination. Others will look at dictatorship and immediately think fear, or that I'm angry with them, because they're more on the insecure side. It's amazing when you think about it from a behavioural perspective, because somewhere on that continuum is a balanced point.

My job, and yours too, is to figure out where I need to land on the continuum for each of those employees in a separate and unique way.

SEVENTEEN

Opinion vs Feedback

It's important to know the difference between opinion and feedback. Opinion is when you provide someone with insights based on your own values. Feedback is based on the values of the receiver. A lot of leaders don't understand why there's a disconnection; they believe it's constructive feedback, but it's actually their opinion.

DISTINGUISHING OPINION FROM FEEDBACK

Many times, you'll find that certain leaders will say (and even believe) that they're giving constructive feedback, when they're actually voicing their opinions. Our personal opinions don't matter, because feedback is not about us. If the behaviours that my employees demonstrate link to a specific task where the outcome was not as optimal as it should have been, then *that* is what I want to provide constructive feedback on, in order to improve an outcome. That is constructive feedback. Whether or not I 'liked' how they did something is irrelevant, as long as it didn't have a negative impact on behaviour, their team, the company, or financials.

The shittiest of bosses are the ones who let their personal opinion of someone affect their rating or review. Those bosses who, even when you did everything correctly (and actually better than they might have thought to do it) remain critical. You hit it out of the park, but because, personally, they don't care for you, they're going to rate your performance as mediocre. And they never make the connection that that is what they've done, because they're shitty leaders.

This takes us back to humility, because really: who are you to be putting your opinions and value judgements on other people? Your personal opinion of your employees is absolutely irrelevant. Who cares? It is your responsibility to treat them fairly and equitably. How I personally feel about people shouldn't matter. As a non-shitty leader, I should be able to recognise that.

Throughout my career, over the thousands of people I've led, there were, of course, many who, on a personal level, I didn't agree with. People I downright didn't like. People who were outwardly homophobic, completely misogynistic, bigoted — things that go against my personal beliefs completely.

But they were not bringing those beliefs into the workforce. They were not bullying or being negative within the work environment. I just happened to know their personal feelings. They were not people I would want to associate with outside of the work place, but, they were the best people for the job and therefore they got that promotion — because they deserved it, based on their outputs. They were my responsibility to support, so I did. Fairly and equitably.

> **When we come to a place of our own authenticity, and we are trying to do right for our team and be kind, what we instantly recognise is that our personal opinion doesn't matter.**

That's when we become comfortable editing ourselves to not share it, because it wasn't asked for, or it's not relevant. How *I* personally feel about the problem you want me to coach you on is absolutely irrelevant. How I personally feel about my staff is also irrelevant. I don't need to like someone that I support through leadership in order to not be a shitty leader. I can be an amazing leader to someone I don't personally like, because how I personally feel should never come into the equation.

When it comes to specific instances, opinion tends to be all about *my* thoughts on a situation. It isn't feedback; it's judgement or observation that, in the end, isn't of much help to your team. Usually, opinion is shared because it feels good for you, the sharer, not because it's of any benefit to the receiver.

For example, imagine someone turns to you and casually says, "Oh. Have you put some weight on?" That is an example of unhelpful, opinion-oriented 'feedback'. But, of course, it's not feedback, because it's not helpful at all. Do you think I'm stupid and don't know I've put on weight? Or do you just feel good calling out someone else's flaws? More importantly, do you think I need the reminder? Maybe I have gained weight, and maybe I don't care. If I don't care that I've gained weight, why do you care? They might say, "Oh, well, I care about your health." Really? If you cared about my mental health, you wouldn't have just called me fat, in so many words.

A similar trend is hiding criticism behind 'jokes'. "Oh, I'm just joking." Really? Jokes are supposed to be funny for all parties involved. Guess what? I'm not laughing. If you feel compelled to say something 'funny' and you're not sure if you should, that uncertainty is your sign to think before speaking.

Feedback is based on the value for the receiver, so you've got to look through the receiver's lens and try to give them what they need. If I'm coaching a client with weight issues, I won't say, "Oh, good morning, Janet. You look like you've put weight on."

It's not me being kind in any way, shape, or form. Now, if Janet comes in and sees me once a month and says, "Oh, Mark. I think I've gained weight," that's different. Then I can say, "Okay, let's focus on why. I'm not worried about the number. I'm concerned about how you feel, and if you're going to beat yourself up over a number, that's an issue for another time. What I'm curious to know is: what is going on in your life right now, and how are you feeling that might have impacted on your ability to lose weight?"

Opinion focuses on your own thoughts and feelings about a situation. Feedback focuses on the behaviours of the receiver. What needs to change for them to improve? What needs to remain the same? What can you say to help them grow? It's about them; it's not about you.

JUDGEMENT AS AN OPINION

Imposing unsolicited opinions on your staff is really casting judgement, which only incites fear, toxicity, shame and blame. This acts as a disabler to corporate culture awareness and non-shitty leadership. We don't come to work to be judged. Constructive feedback is designed to develop and inspire someone to improve behaviour, to create a different outcome. Judgement does the inverse of that. Feedback has a goal, an output to improve. Opinion just makes you feel better because you're hearing yourself talk.

Sometimes I'm labelled as intimidating (which I have always found quite humorous) because I speak my mind. I will call people out respectfully. If someone gives an opinion, I'll simply remind them that an opinion provided unsolicited is a judgement.

I will still be kind about it. Again, being kind versus right doesn't mean you can't tell people when you're annoyed or frustrated with them. You can display emotion. You can say, "I'm feeling this right now, so I'm going to step outside for a few minutes. When I'm finished, I'll come back and have a chat with you." I'm being kind, because I'm choosing not to whine, yell or moan. This is taking control of your emotions.

There is something to be said about having the courage to keep your mouth shut. It's just a matter of thinking, "What is the intention of my conversation?" Healthy communication is about intention. "Why are you telling me this? Why do I need to know and why should I care?" Are you telling me this because you want to rile me? Are you telling me this because you want to be right? Are you telling me this because I need to know, and you're being kind in telling me?

When someone is telling me something because they want to be right, I won't engage with it. If they feel the need to be right, they can go and be right somewhere else. If they're telling me because they're trying to be cheeky, and they're being passive aggressive, then I'll probably call them out on that. "Did you want to share that with me because you wanted me to react this way, or is there something else underlying here that you'd like to talk about? Because I'm happy to have an adult conversation with you."

There are a lot of people who try to voice their opinion without saying that's what they're doing, but you can always tell that they have these hidden agendas. The hidden agendas are based on their opinions. This really doesn't have a place in the workplace; it's damaging. When people are giving opinions in the workplace instead of feedback, others feel as though they're being judged, and that's when they're going to be defensive. A judgemental workforce is usually the catalyst for more shitty leadership.

HONEST FEEDBACK MEANS TRUE HUMILITY

Have you ever noticed that we tend to discount the compliments we receive? And we usually do so because we're expected to. If someone says, "You have a beautiful home" and you reply, "Why yes, I do!" it's often seen as arrogant. But why is that? Why is it bad to acknowledge good things? Why is it that we're deemed narcissistic or arrogant or cocky or whatever the adjective *du jour* is for people when we proclaim our strengths?

In one-on-ones with new people I will often ask, "Tell me something you're really good at." It makes people so bloody uncomfortable! They squirm, they stutter, they often flat-out can't respond at all. People don't like talking about their strengths. And yet we find it so easy to focus on our weaknesses.

We discount compliments and fear constructive criticism.

This is where humility goes out the window, people confuse self-deprecation with humility. But humility is simply understanding that you're never going to be perfect. Self-deprecation is ignoring and downplaying your strengths, which is not humble and helps no one.

True vulnerability means being able to easily produce a list of six things you're really good at, as well as six things you need to improve on. Showing vulnerability and humility works both ways.

If you, as a leader, aren't really tuned into what true humility is, you won't be able to recognise it in your employees. You might see someone who is self-deprecating as either being humble or insecure. And then you're giving them your opinion on it, rather than feedback. There are lots of misperceptions floating around the workforce, because those who are insecure think confident people are narcissists, while the confident ones think the insecure people are weak. So, it becomes this cat and mouse game, and no one improves; it's all based on a misperception and a disconnection between the way I see myself and the way others see me, which is the foundation for the Ego Continuum.

> Great feedback starts with true humility.

WHAT REAL FEEDBACK LOOKS LIKE

True feedback is both positive and constructive, delivered in a format that is best for the employee receiving it. Feedback dialogue should be balanced. It should be in the form of a series of questions, where the employee can reach a conclusion himself or herself. You could also signpost how you're going to jointly solve any problems together.

"Could you suggest some ways in which you could have done this differently? You understand that the outcome was this, but I needed it to be this, so how can we help each other so that you get to this level? What can you do differently? What could you try right now, on your next call, in your next meeting, with this client, or with this initiative?" Good feedback asks those kinds of questions.

If you use these techniques and approach these sessions with your employees in a deliberate, conscious way and try to come up with solutions together, this will help you to avoid opinion.

Effective feedback also needs to be coupled with lens awareness, and all the other stuff we've covered so far. Your lens affects your feedback. What if you've got a confident employee working for an insecure shitty leader, who has no self-awareness? That confidence is going to be misconstrued and shot down. But if you're engaging in all of this while practising effective feedback, it really creates a workplace where communication flows easily. There's a fluidity to the way effective communication drives non-shitty leadership behaviours, and it's beneficial for all involved.

This is really about putting your money where your mouth is. You're confident with the first pillar: you've identified who you are through self-awareness. You've started marketing your leadership brand through that development. Effective feedback delivery is actually putting that into action.

INSTIGATE, INITIATE, IGNITE

Self-awareness instigates. Your leadership brand initiates. Effective feedback ignites.

Self-awareness instigates the leader to initiate the art of non-shitty leadership. The instigation is the leader learning about them.

My leadership brand initiates me to be able to share what I have recognised about myself, and put into action who I want to be as a leader. I have to recognise who I am versus how you see me, which is the Ego Continuum in itself.

Ignition is setting the stage for the journey we are taking together. I know who I am. I know *you* know who I am. And now you know how to react to me; if I'm not acting like myself, instead of thinking of me as a shitty leader, you'll help me recognise what I'm doing. You'll manage up and help me get back on track, and then we can avoid all the unnecessary rubbish, which is why there's a global epidemic. That employee/leader connection naturally leads to feedback for you. We're a team. There's alignment if this feedback is effective. I'm aligned with myself. I'm aligned with you. We're aligned together. And that creates a truly harmonious workplace.

REVIEWING 'WHAT' AND 'HOW' BEHAVIOURS

The main components of effective feedback delivery are to make it unique, bespoke and specific for the individuals involved. It is not about providing the experience for your team. It's about giving each of them what they need to help them be more successful in their role.

For example, imagine that Janet needs to improve her Excel skills. She has to run pivot tables on a regular basis, but she doesn't know pivot tables well. So, I send her on a course, or I provide her with a mentor who's got really sharp Excel skills, and Janet masters it. However, she continually makes a mistake with one bit in particular, which then alters the pivot table. And now, I have to give her that feedback.

She's made a valiant effort, but if I don't say anything, she won't improve. So, there's a specific 'what', or a 'what' behaviour. It's a tangible specific; a skill or outcome that needs improving.

There are also the 'how' behaviours. Four different people mentored Janet. They all showed her different skills and tricks to help her master Excel. However, she was incredibly belligerent. She was rude. She wasn't thankful or grateful in demonstrating anything to the people who took time out of their schedules to mentor her. And now she's actually talking about them behind their backs.

Those are 'how' behaviours that also warrant feedback. It's not *what* she needs to learn; it's *how* she's accomplished it. If you're not performance managing your staff based on the what and the how, then in both of those scenarios, the outcome of Janet's performance review would be great. She'd be a rock star, because the goal was to improve her Excel skills, which she did. At one point, I had to remind her of something. It was one piece, which is fine; we're all human. And she actually improved and did a great job. If I hadn't looked at the 'how' behaviours and only focused on the 'what', then Janet in my second example would still be considered a rock star. It wouldn't matter that she had upset her mentors.

Sometimes, there are perceptions that salespeople will use unethical practices in order to generate sales, or won't follow process. First, I would look at the sales targets and examine how fear is used to manage people, because some people live in constant fear that if they don't make their quota two months in a row, they're going to lose their job. So, come hell or high water, they will make their quota, even if they're engaged in things that are unethical. Then again, some salespeople are doing unethical things for other reasons, and you have to address that behaviour.

Yet, some organisations choose to ignore these behaviours. Unless they're looking at the 'what' and the 'how,' they're missing 50% of the problem that, again, is a contributor to shitty leadership. I've had employees who hit their numbers on everything and therefore rated themselves exceptional, but were corporate bullies — rude, belligerent and spreading toxicity. But because we were only rating them on the 'what' and not the 'how,' I couldn't really comment on their behaviours, because I was told that this was subjective. It was my opinion. It wasn't really constructive feedback, so they were still rated exceptional, because their target was to hit XYZ, and they did hit XYZ. How they got there was irrelevant — because it wasn't documented in the actual objective.

Feedback has to consider the 'how', or your workplace will suffer due to behavioural inconsistencies.

RECAP

Effective feedback is not an opinion. It's not casting unsolicited judgement. It has specific goals in mind; it's for the receiver, not for you. Opinion is based on you; feedback is based on them. Their needs. Their desires. Their strengths. What they need to do to change a specific behaviour. It's not about sharing your opinions to no effect; it's to help them improve, and should be delivered in a way that will do this. It focuses on the 'what' and the 'how' behaviours, because the 'how' behaviours affect the workplace just as much as the 'what.'

EIGHTEEN

Your Ego Continuum

This is the final section; we will review the framework for how we put it all together. If you think about where you are in your own Ego Continuum, if you recognise the three elements of active leadership and if you are aligned on your frequency, you're well on your way to becoming a non-shitty leader. You recognise that some of it is going to feel uncomfortable with that disruptive lens — this is where you can get to leadership by exception.

THE BENEFITS OF NON-SHITTY LEADERSHIP

The context of leadership by exception is this: consider a shitty environment as compared to a non-shitty environment. In a shitty environment, you're managing the costs of working for a disengaged workforce, unnatural attrition, people quitting and staying and continued rework. Things are just not going the way they're supposed to go, because people aren't communicating. People feel like shit and receive inconsistent or no feedback. There is no plan or mandate to help anyone improve. People are not the focus.

Compare that to a non-shitty environment, where 80% of your leaders are aligned. There is bespoke feedback. There is continued concentration on what needs to be done from a clear, concise priorities perspective, so there's a limited or highly reduced amount of rework. There is a plan! There is an ability just to go and actively lead. When I am doing that consciously, when I am aware of my surroundings and I am actively leading my teams, I really only have to manage the highs and lows, aka the 'exceptions,' because all the nonsense, noise and craziness that happened before has actually stopped.

Think about an environment where 20 leaders are all more self-aware. They each recognise their frequency and work together from a place of being kind instead of needing to be right. Everyone has released their ego, knows where they sit on the Ego Continuum and recognises its fluidity. Everyone has a feedback mindset, which has led to a culture of feedback. It's a safe and nurturing environment where vulnerability is seen as a strength. Everyone in leadership has asked the two questions, so feedback is delivered in a way that changes the outcomes for the better.

People like coming to work. Sunday despair goes away. There is no blame and shame. People are not afraid to ask questions and manage up. Their customers start to notice it, because employees are engaged and happy. They feel aligned, valued and respected. They're in the moment and they are self-motivated. They're inspired because everyone recognises that they're all in this together. It feels like a democracy, but when dictatorship needs to happen, people just get it done, and then celebrate their wins.

This time, when Billy messes up and it affects a customer, I can kick in and say, "Billy, listen. Don't beat yourself up over it. This is an exception. How do we fix it?" I guarantee you, Billy has already taken every accountability to fix it.

As a leader, and from a return on investment perspective, how much have I now saved as a result of this methodology at work through 80% of my staff? I can now focus on my own development, which I have neglected before. I can focus on the critical things like succession planning, disaster recovery and business contingency. Maybe I can start to look at some wellness issues to help bring a body/mind/soul connection to this environment. I can continue to work on my links and relationships, and make sure that all of the work we've done has now transitioned to a culture of feedback and alignment. Now I have the time to work towards sustaining this new culture, engage in process improvement and continue to make this even better.

CONNECTING, REINFORCING AND MAINTAINING THE EGO CONTINUUM

To really get to that place — to reap all those benefits — the next step is connecting, reinforcing and maintaining your Ego Continuum in light of everything you've learned so far. One of the simplest ways to do this, to unite all of this, is to pay it forward.

The challenge that I set for every person that reads this book is to go and mentor someone that *doesn't* report to you. Mentor a peer, colleague or boss. Give them your copy of the book, or buy them a new one, and pay it forward. Share what you've learned. Help someone else recognise their value and where they are on their own Ego Continuum. Help reduce the global epidemic of shitty leadership.

Remember what it felt like when you first understood you were demonstrating shitty leadership behaviours? Think back to the day where you had the epiphany, when you realised that some of your behaviours incited feelings of shame and despair in others. If humility is the greatest skill that any leader can demonstrate, then true humility is being that support when you see someone else have the same epiphany. Help them move through it; help them let go of shame and grow.

The next step towards connecting all of this is to consistently track your frequency alignment. Earlier, we talked about self-awareness. We talked about the ability to find and maintain your frequency. Months from now, what will you be doing about it? Will you still be tracking it? How will you have curbed your negative thinking?

Have you ever had one of those days where you just feel like you're in a shitty mood, and you don't know why? As soon as you feel that way, stop what you're doing. Ask yourself: *"Why am I anxious?"* or *"Why am I angry?"* Try to figure it out. That is how to find and maintain your frequency.

Some people don't realise that they're in a shitty mood by choice. They think they're in a bad mood because someone incited it in them. You choose how you feel. You choose how you think, therefore you choose your actions, and your behaviour. If that choice is difficult, that's when you stop and realign. Changing your outlook or sense of perspective has a huge impact on the way you interact with the world.

I have found that when we authentically engage, we will be accountable for our thoughts, feelings, behaviours and emotions. This approach holds you to a higher standard, ensuring that when you start emitting the behavioural outputs of a shitty leader, you can catch and fix them. Part of recognising your current brand is learning how to become self-aware, and understanding how your team's peers and even your own boss, has perceived you. The shadows that you cast can be found by simply having conversations with others or sometimes conversations with yourself. Are you intuitive enough to read your own non-verbal signs? Can you also provide feedback forums that are confidential? Can you talk to your HR department about offering a 360-feedback review? If you have an honest team that feels safe providing truthful feedback without fear of retaliation, then you will instantly learn what you leave behind; the shadows you cast.

If you're a positive, fair leader and great at delivering feedback, you will leave behind an air of equality and support. Your team should have no issue with telling you the truth. If you're a shitty leader, on the other hand, you'll find that you're leaving behind a path of fear, toxicity, frustration and apathy.

> **What current culture do your actions and behaviours create?**

RIGHT VS KIND BAROMETER

Think about a time when you were arguing with someone else: did you want to be right just to prove a point? Just to be right for the sake of being right? Then, honestly, why bother? Why do you have a need to be right? As a leader, are you so insecure that you have to prove yourself, right? How is that affecting the way your team perceives you, or contributing to the culture? It's a shitty behaviour. You won't be trusted, because you don't provide a safe environment for the team.

The concept of right versus kind is the cornerstone of the Ego Continuum. In any situation, you've got a choice to make. Do you want to be right, or do you want to be kind? One outcome has a more productive output. If I'm trying to curb behaviour through constructive feedback and want to 'catch' that person because I personally don't like them, then I'm making it about me. I'm sharing my opinion versus feedback, and I'm not setting my employee up to succeed. I'm basically going, "Na-na, na-na-na. You were wrong!" That is a shitty leader; you're not motivating and inspiring. You're being childlike.

Do you ever get into an argument with someone and then forget why you're arguing; yet you still do it? Do you talk over people because you just want to be heard? You know the conversation is going to become heated, so you start to speak over the person because you want to make your point? Such egocentric moments are not about fixing a problem; they create more of a problem.

When you're trying to deliver constructive feedback, you want to do it from a place of kindness. If it is someone you don't like, you can still be kind to them.

If you choose kindness, does that mean you're always wrong? No, it doesn't. It simply forces you to assess: why did you want to be right in the first place? Is it because you wanted the other person to be wrong? In terms of this being connected to the Ego Continuum, if you're busy trying to be right, there's no way you can place yourself on the continuum. You're not inwardly focused enough. If you want to constantly be right, then you're going to be perceived as narcissistic, which means you're probably outside your leadership brand, and this means you're not getting it.

If I am trying to provide a bespoke level of feedback that is constructive, that changes the behaviours of my staff in order to create different outcomes, then regardless of whether they want me to be democratic or a dictator, my first approach is: how do I deliver this feedback? How do I come across as being kind, so that the message is heard? Because when I come across as wanting to be right, I will put the individual on the defensive, which then puts me on the offensive, which we don't need. It is counterproductive to delivering constructive feedback. It's not constructive at all.

Kindness is a way of making sure that things are tailored to each individual person. Kindness creates and builds a connection, which is what this is all about. If you think back to the story of my supervisor who stopped talking to me to 'punish' me, that's an example of someone choosing to be right instead of kind. Their actions were about them. They were not productive in the slightest. They wanted to punish me, rather than actually try and improve my behaviours. They didn't care about being kind or changing any outputs; they wanted to be right.

ARE YOU SELF-AWARE ENOUGH TO KNOW YOU'RE SELF-AWARE?

At this point, if you're putting all of this into practice and you don't see any progress or change, then I would question your ability to reflect and to be self-aware. Maybe you haven't gone deep enough. Being self-aware means being authentically engaged, being accountable to emotions, forcing yourself to a higher standard and being aware of who you're talking to and how you're coming across.

You have to be authentic to know how you're going to come across. If you like someone personally, then it's easier to find that ability. It's when you *don't* like them that you have to be careful. It's really about that level of planning.

I'm not trying to solve a global epidemic with perfection. I'm trying to solve it through realness and authenticity. People should always, first and foremost, be themselves. That being said, if you're naturally a dictator, then you've got some work to do. If you're naturally someone who is egocentric and narcissistic and wants to constantly be right, then I would question why you're in leadership. And are you truly narcissistic, or are your insecurities rearing their heads and you're being misperceived as narcissistic?

Real-time, honest thinking means that you're aware of how you're thinking. You make choices consciously, and you own your thoughts. You're accountable for your emotions. When you stop lying to yourself and thinking about the way you need to be for others, and are being who you are instead, your authentic self will emerge. When it does, you just make that connection. Then it all seems to fall into place. You find your frequency, and you know how to stay on it. You identify an ability to create your leadership brand. Then you build it, you share it, and you own it. You've created an environment where people are now free to manage up, and you respect it because they respect you.

Recognise in yourself what you expect in others, and then simply go ahead and do it. Lead by example, so that you can help reduce the global epidemic of today.

RECAP

The benefits of non-shitty leadership are many, and the ROI is significant. But to keep moving forward with this process, you have to connect everything you've learned with your own Ego Continuum. That involves paying it forward by mentoring someone else in this process. It also involves tracking with your own frequency, and continually choosing to be kind over right. It involves consistently checking in with your own self-awareness, because it's only through self-awareness that you can grow and have a positive impact on your team, and on the global epidemic of shitty leaders.

NINETEEN

ROI: Exception Management & Time Savings

When you have an engaged workforce, you only have to manage highs and lows. You focus on the bottom 20% and the top goals, including strategy, succession planning and career development. Remember, the value of an engaged workforce has been documented, and it is incredibly high. What's more, a disengaged workforce will cost you much more than you probably want to pay!

SOME STATISTICS

Remember at the beginning of the book we shared, 75% of US workers cite their boss as the biggest cause of stress at work, but the majority (59%) of workers with a poor manager still don't leave. A mere 21% of employees say their performance is managed in a way that motivates them to do outstanding work. 42% believe their accomplishments go unnoticed and the same percentage feel that executive leadership does not contribute to a positive company culture. A whopping 84% of employees are looking for year-round, in the moment feedback! Are they getting it?

As you continue this work, remember what you're working for. Keep in mind that all of this has a direct effect on the profitability success of your company.

ROI AND COST SAVINGS

An engaged workforce flows smoothly because everyone is aligned. Everyone is informed. Everyone is valued. People just come to work, and they enjoy what they're doing, and they know their leader has their back. They know their leader will catch them doing things right and not try to set them up to fail. They have a clear direction and know that they'll get feedback. They know they can manage up. They understand your leadership brand. Everybody has an interest in wanting to do what is kind, so that things just flow. There is less friction. There is a distinct path. Everyone's continuum is aligned and running in parallel.

When everyone is focused on maintaining an active frequency, then everyone's frequency is aligned. At that point, when toxicity attempts to enter the engaged workforce, people don't allow it. They stop it before it spreads, because they remember how things used to be, and they don't want a repeat of that. If some gossipy, backstabbing employee suddenly came on board, the workplace culture wouldn't support it.

There are many ways that companies can measure the costs and rewards at this point; it just depends on what's important to them. They can look at the impact of sales over the last 12 months. They can look at their cost of rework and the reductions in rework. How many clients did they lose in this 12-month period versus the last 12-month period, and what's different?

What are their customers saying? There is no greater feedback. What are their internal employee survey scores? How have those improved over the last six to 12 months? On those confidential surveys, employees will normally tell the truth.

When everything is going right, then the exceptions become fewer and fewer, so there is much more constructive activity going on in the workplace. Things don't seem as catastrophic as they did before.

RECAP

The stats show that investing in non-shitty leadership pays for itself, many times over. You start with that self-awareness journey; you look inside yourself and get firmly on your road. Then you learn about your triggers, and how you can make choices. Then, you develop your ability to recognise your behaviours and why certain triggers can make you react the way you do. Then, regarding your reactions, you make sure to choose kindness over being right. Finally, you balance your reactions to maintain focus in real time.

In terms of dealing with employees, you have to continue to elicit the kind of feedback they want, and ask them how they want to be led. You spot check. If you have a good rapport with them, they will keep you abreast of what's happening in their life. If the last time you asked the two questions was 1986, I would say that you are probably a little overdue in asking them again! To keep getting the exception management time-savings, you have to continue to apply this actively. That's why it's called *active* leadership!

You have to be active and in the moment. If, six months ago, everything was fine, and now your employee is going through a divorce, or they've been sick and they're returning to work, things will be different. Things they cared about before, when you asked those questions, might not be the same things they care about now. Without getting too personal, those are the things you need to know, because that's going to change your approach.

TWENTY

"Happiness is the new rich. Inner peace is the new success. Health is the new wealth. Kindness is the new cool." — *Unknown.*

Putting It All Together

The end goal of becoming savvy with the Ego Continuum, to understanding your continuum and all you've learned, is this: recognise the sense of empowerment in the time you get back, now that you can lead so much more efficiently. In this chapter, we'll review the basics of what we've covered, tie it all together and leave you with practical, actionable steps you can take today in order to become a non-shitty leader.

A RECAP TO TIE IT ALL TOGETHER

By becoming self-aware, by acting on that self-awareness, being constructive, and letting go of being right, you will feel inner peace. You will feel happiness. You will feel a sense of well-being.

> When things are simple, it all just works.

We start with the disengaged workforce. What is the cost of disengagement within your organisation? This can be demonstrated by things like unnatural attrition, absenteeism, and impacts from poor communication, corporate bullying, misaligned perceptions and poor leadership. Then we discuss times when a shitty leader has led you.

The next step is the uncomfortable realisation that you may have demonstrated some of these behaviours, and now you see the impacts of these on the feelings and actions of others. Then we move into that feeling, and that concept of innovative disruption. This is the introduction to a possible new way of thinking, a new lens, and you learn that what you uncover through reflections may feel uncomfortable, and that's okay. You learn how to accept your past behaviours and work towards improvement.

Now you move forward, and you've got your shame and forgiveness in the forward lens. Shame can be a normal by-product when reflecting on your past shitty behaviours. Don't spend too much time self-deprecating. Make peace and learn to use your forward lens through innovative disruption awareness. Then you delve into your Ego Continuum, and that is the difference between how you see yourself versus how others see you. This is where we talk about perception management. Then we get into true self-awareness and reflection. Are you self-aware enough to know you're self-aware? How do you know? Are you honest with yourself when reflecting, and are you sure?

We then get into frequency awareness and maintenance. This is the concept of how to engage self-awareness by frequency awareness and ownership, using your energy wisely and reflecting more deeply on those times when you reacted in a certain way, and learning how to use a different lens to alter those perceptions. You learned about your triggers, and how different words can incite how we choose to feel and react to certain situations. One of the largest catalysts here is the feeling of being a victim, which leads us to our chosen victim state. Sometimes we find comfort in playing the victim role, which can lead to perceived shitty leadership or inappropriate behaviours. It's all about learning how to train yourself to react differently to situations in real time and not accepting the emotional connections from others who are playing the victim, so you become one too.

This is when we get into your power of choice, and the reminder that you always have a choice in how you feel, react and respond to certain situations. The victim choice is also a choice, so learn how to choose an alternative.

Now we move into authentic vulnerability. Through learning or unlearning things about you, you're holding up a mirror. Through vulnerability, you can tap into your unknown strengths, as vulnerability is, in itself, strength. That leads to perception management, and you tie it all together through your revised self-awareness lens and how you can remain in control of your thoughts, feelings, actions and reactions and demonstrate effective leadership behaviours.

You're then ready to create your leadership brand. What is your leadership style? How do you want to be seen as a leader? What does working for you mean for your staff? What aspects of your leadership behaviours are you willing to declare up front to avoid unnecessary misperceptions and help your staff to help hold you accountable?

Now we've moved into effective feedback delivery. Use the two questions and engage in effective conversations. Share specifics about their demonstrated behaviours, and together determine how best to improve these behaviours for the next time. It's not about opinion. It's about constructive feedback to change an outcome based on demonstrated behaviours. How you feel is irrelevant. Deliver it in the best way for them. It's not about you. Get to this stage, and we now can lead by exception. We reach this stage when 80% of your team are realigned, refocused, and feel supported in ways that are best for them, due to your new-found lens awareness through your Ego Continuum development. When you reach this level, you should be spending less time in the daily weeds, as most things now just have a flow to them. Engagement ensues, and you spend your time on the exceptional highs and lows.

Finally, you are now able to really see the benefits of an engaged workforce. You can now see all of the changes that have occurred in the six to 12 months, and make an end comparison between where you and your organisation were at the start of this journey and where you are now. What are you noticing? What return on investment gains have you received? Reduced customer complaints, more customer satisfaction, reduced unnatural employee attrition? Less fear, less quit and stay, increased engagement? Reductions in rework, improved communication and more time for you to spend developing your staff? All of those things will start to come naturally.

THE JOYS OF AN ENGAGED WORKFORCE

I find that in non-shitty leadership environments, the relationship between the employee and the leader has a very strong non-verbal communication approach. With just one look, you can tell what the other is thinking. It develops a connection to the point where you can complete each other's sentences; it creates a relationship! It creates a partnership, not unlike a partnership in life. People joke about their work spouses, but that's exactly what this is. In this environment, people think, "*I get you. I feel connected to you because I understand what you're all about. I know you're not trying to be rude. I know you're not trying to set me up to fail. I know you care about me doing things right. You set me up to succeed. Therefore, I make you succeed.*"

This is where it goes beyond leadership. This whole methodology of everything we've talked about, from start to finish, doesn't just change how you're perceived as a leader — it can change your life. Because when you become truly self-grounded, you know who you are, and you just live your life. No games. No false expectations. You don't pretend to be something you're not. You understand basic human connection, and you recognise that you're worthy of that connection.

It's pure, it's true and it's honest. It's uncomplicated, it's simplistic and it's natural. It just is.

No games. It's not about ego and being right. It's not about needing to be number one. It's "You be you, and I'll be me. Let's figure out how we can do that in harmony." If it just so happens that there is an employee/leader relationship, then we figure out the best way to make that work. Then we just go and do it, because at the end of the day, work is work — but isn't it everything outside of that work time that should really, truly be the priority?

No one's epitaph would ever say, "Man. I wish I'd spent more time at the office."

LEADERSHIP BY EXCEPTION: THE FOUR COMPONENTS

The main goal of this whole journey is to have 80% of your employee activity running smoothly; that's an engaged workforce. Then your leadership is all about managing the exceptions: the remaining 20% of highs and lows.

Remember the four components? That's how we get to leadership by exception. These are the Ego Continuum, Active Leadership, Frequency Awareness and Innovative Disruption.

The Ego Continuum is the perception management piece. You have to first perceive what the continuum is, and then place yourself on it. It's the difference between how you see yourself and how others see you. It's that continuum of narcissism versus insecurity. Somewhere in that sliding scale is your leadership brand. All of this is covered extensively in Book One.

Active leadership in and of itself is made up of three pillars: self-awareness, leadership brand and effective feedback delivery.

Frequency awareness is recognising how to become self-aware and taking ownership of your thoughts and feelings. It's that whole piece of work we did about behaviours, triggers and recognising the power of choice. It's about realising that your frequency is something you can manage and maintain. If you envision this road, you stay on it, and you don't let the energy vampires attack you, then you can choose how you think and feel.

Innovative Disruption is when all of this starts to feel uncomfortable. Embrace the fact that this is where change occurs and recognise that you are enough. Now you just have to believe it — and act on it.

It's truly not caring what other people think; not just saying that you don't care, but truly believing it. That's pretty important, comparing one person to another is apples and oranges. Each of us is unique.

Everything you're doing here, as you grow in this self-awareness and connection, is going to carry over into every aspect of your life. It's going to help with all your relationships, not just your work life.

SOME PRACTICAL STEPS AS YOU MOVE FORWARD

In Section 2, you began your journey into self-awareness; this insight leads to the power of vulnerability, if you're comfortable enough to access it. Once you do, you can choose to share some of these insights with others around you. Our staff benefit from our own reflections and experiences. Sharing is a good thing.

The next piece goes more into detail about self-awareness; this is where we get into feelings and triggers. The most important step here is to really figure out and understand what your triggers are; your personal examples and reflection will help you discover this. Link the power and influence that victim-like words have on us. Practise identifying triggers in real time, so you are choosing exactly how you want to respond.

Section 3 got us thinking about our leadership brand. Make sure you take the time to create a unique and authentic leadership brand, and learn how to share it effectively. As you begin to effectively manoeuvre in a branded environment, you will have more and more ability to proactively reduce and control misperceptions of shitty leadership through vulnerability and authenticity.

As you move on and learn effective feedback delivery, you'll discover how to engage everyone as individuals. Although there are always similarities to feedback delivery, the audience for the feedback differs and must be tailored to them. Feedback is intended to develop; not prosecute or persecute. Learn the difference between opinion versus feedback and how most have been confusing it for years. Remember that opinion comes from your own lens, which, in a feedback discussion, is unnecessary.

Then, as we mentioned before, the most effective action step you can take to really tie all this together is to find a person to mentor. This can be a peer, a team member, or even a boss — and that's where you can practise managing up!

As you mentor and grow yourself, you'll soon understand how to link these frameworks together: The Ego Continuum, Active Leadership, Frequency Awareness and Innovative Disruption. That's when you'll discover that ideal state of leadership by exception.

CONTINUING COMMUNITY

As you continue with this work, part of the process is finding others to connect with. A book is just one isolated lesson — a community is what really helps you grow. That's why we've created a closed Facebook group, and we hope you'll join us there, wherever you are on your journey. You can find this group through our website (www.ego-continuum.co.uk) or our Facebook page (https://www.facebook.com/egocontinuum/), and that's where you'll be able to go in and comment on topics, start your own discussions or talk to others around the globe who have found their journey through the Ego Continuum. This is the start of making a real difference; a dent in the global epidemic of shitty leadership. Come and join us.

TWENTY-ONE

Leading Resistant Employees

This is the what's next. You've done it all. Changed your lens. Become more self-aware. You have a brand that most of your employees are on board with. But you still have one or two employees who can't get past your past shitty behaviours. Now what do you do? How can you, as the newfound non-shitty leader, help them become more receptive to what you are now attempting to do and achieve? Or what if the coin is flipped — what if you've become an amazing leader, but are still struggling with how you treat your boss? Are *you* the resistant employee?

REVISITING LEADERSHIP BY EXCEPTION

Remember that leadership by exception means that 80% of your team is humming along smoothly. They've taken really well to this active leadership thing. And you're left to lead the exceptions. Half of these are highs; this is the good stuff, the planning for succession and leadership/staff development. But the other half are lows — the 10%. The employees that just don't want to get on board. Those are the exceptions. Those are the outliers.

Now, some of these exceptions aren't necessarily doing anything wrong. They're just not being dynamic employees. Some of them maybe *are* doing something wrong. They might be openly resisting this new culture. That may be the way they've always been, or they may have been moulded and incited by your past shitty behaviours to expect — and contribute to — a shitty environment. It's time for you to own that.

THE EMPLOYEE BRAND

If you can lead yourself effectively, then you can lead others. Every employee can be leading themselves via their own active employee framework; self-awareness, employee brand and receiving feedback.

Some of the resistant employees have been on the receiving end of feeling blame and shame from a variety of leaders, so they will generally not trust leaders at all. In some instances, it's not the shitty leader who is at fault; they might not be accountable for the way the inactive employee is feeling. But you can at least help the employee get to a place where they not only recognise their own self-awareness, but start to recognise their employee brand. Is the brand naturally distrusting? Is that who they want to be?

When talking about employee brand, make sure there's context. You have a context for the leadership brand and a step-by-step on how to build that. They don't have that for employee brand, so that is something you'll need to extrapolate for them.

An employee brand, like a leadership brand, involves perception management: how do you want to be defined as an employee? What are your preferred learning styles? What is your level of trust and engagement? How ambitious are you? How do you want to be perceived by your leadership team? Some people just want to go to work and come home; they don't care about promotions. You know what? That's part of their brand, and that's okay. Not everybody aspires to a leadership role. I believe that if you declare that upfront, it will help people understand. Just like talking about leadership skills. You can demonstrate leadership skills in a non-leadership role. It doesn't mean you want to be a leader, but you can show strength, determination, courage and command, and be an excellent employee.

There's a lot to think about here, but the key issue is trust. Employee brand is *how willing you are to trust*. What is your trust engagement? If you're the active leader of an inactive employee, how are you going to win back their trust?

Find the catalyst for why they're not letting down their guard.

Does it have anything to do with you as a leader, or is it related to something completely outside your control?

THE RESISTANT EMPLOYEE

This is where you need to reflect and analyse. Some of your employee's behaviour can be linked to how you were in the past. Some of them just won't want to change; they want things to be the way they've always been. If they have been on the residual end of working in a toxic culture for many, many years, it will be very challenging to unlearn their own behaviours. But unlearning is exactly what has to happen.

Behaviour is not innate. Behaviours are chosen. Personality is who you are, behaviour is what you do. If it's something you do, you have control over it, so you can change it. The problem is, some people get so comfortable in their behaviours that these become memorised.

It's called conditional automatic functioning. It's like when you drive a car and you get home and you realise, "*Oh, I'm home already.*" You don't remember driving all the way. You just did it. We are creatures of habit, but these are all learned behaviours. The behaviour outputs at work, the way we interact with people, the way we interact with those we haven't liked for years, becomes automatic functioning as well. We will instantly disagree with someone we don't like, just because that's what we're used to doing, or we will instantly become defensive because we think they're going to yell at us, like they used to. It's part of learning. It's recognising that we do this, and then unlearning it in order to be fair to the person who has made an effort to change.

EMPLOYEE TRANSFORMATION

As a leader, a difficult but essential part of your job is continuing to engage in active conversations. You need to remain kind and understanding, and then start a dialogue. Just say, "Hey, what do you think of the changes I've made?"

If you're now comfortable with vulnerability, you will, no doubt, have also declared your leadership brand and trained your staff accordingly, because you hold them accountable to hold you accountable. But if you sensed that they're not getting it or don't care, you need to understand why. Maybe they need to unlearn some behaviours to cut you some slack. Or maybe there's something you haven't done for them. Ask them, "What are some of the things I could do?" That's total vulnerability.

Let's say I have an employee and I've been a shitty leader for five years. Throughout that time, they've reported to me. We've had HR issues. We've had verbal fights, and we just know we don't get along. Now, I come in months later. I've done this shitty leadership course, I've read the books, I've made massive changes and 80% of the staff are on board. But this one individual just does not trust me. We have a discussion where he or she is very vocal and says, "Yeah. I see what you've done. I get your brand, but I'm going to need a lot of time to really ever trust you again because of all the stuff that's happened in the past." Once bitten, twice shy, right?

That's their choice. At the end of the day, you have to start by recognising that there is a problem. Not everyone is going to buy into your shitty leadership revolution, so what are the steps you can take when you recognise that someone is still not fully there?

At this point, do more of the same. Keep being vulnerable; keep initiating that dialogue. Call it out, but lead the employee the way they like to be led and be aware of how they like to receive feedback. As tempting as it will be at times, you can't demand their trust; you have to earn it. So, find out how. You might say, "I'm sensing that there are still some disconnections based on past behaviours. Is it merely a question of time, or are there things you've not said to me that you'd like to? How can we work towards that discussion? How can we get the closure that you need?"

You might find some dissonance between what you think the employee wants and what the employee actually feels.

With dialogue, you can address that. This leads to trust. If a leader thinks an employee needs more managing than they actually do, and that employee just wants them to back off, a vulnerable dialogue could almost certainly address that issue, and you could come to a trust-filled compromise — dissolving that dissonance.

Of course, there will always be employees who aren't receptive, no matter what you do. As said before, repeating the same behaviour and expecting a different outcome is the definition of insanity. If you're engaging in your one-on-ones and using your newfound leadership skills, you will see, in a very short amount of time, who is receptive and who isn't. They might have told you how they like to receive feedback, but they clearly aren't receiving it. They might be arguing with you at every opportunity. They might just be hostile and disgruntled. Whatever form these reactions are taking, the natural progression is to then continue the conversation in a different way with those who are struggling. Simply divert your conversation: "What can I do to help you help me?"

THE LEADER AS A RESISTANT EMPLOYEE

> Now what do you do if this one disgruntled employee — is you?

Most leaders still have bosses to report to. How have you contributed to that relationship? Have you reacted defensively to feedback? Or have you practised managing up in a healthy way?

Just like a shitty leader, remember: a shitty employee is not a shitty person. It just means that they still have shitty behaviours. How receptive are you to feedback? How willing are you to embrace change? If your leader has historically been shitty for the last 20 years and he or she is making an effort, are you cutting them some slack? Are you kind to them in order to give them the ability to win back your trust? Are you noticing and respecting what it is that they're attempting to do? Or are you so caught up in your own negative influences about what they've done in the past that you can't see the forest through the trees?

If you have become a really good, non-shitty leader in every capacity for your staff, but you're still a shitty employee to your own boss, what kind of example are you setting?

Some people might struggle with reflection on an inwards basis, which can set them up for this particular kind of hypocrisy. If they know they're going to be watched because they have to market their leadership brand outwards, they might think, at the onset, that they can fake their way through all this and just go through the motions. But if they're still bad-mouthing their own boss, they're going to undermine their own efforts.

Ask yourself: are you a shitty employee? What are your expectations and outcomes? Are you passionate about what you're doing for a living? If no, why not? Your employee brand is the same as your leadership brand, except for the fact that this is self-leadership. How do you want to be perceived? Are you a dynamic person? Are you someone who likes to self-manage? Are you the kind of person that wants to get lots of guidance? Who are you at work? What do you want to be your best?

What level of engagement do you want from your leader? It means defining what you believe you are responsible and accountable for, versus what your leader is responsible and accountable for.

RECAP

As a leader, you must embrace the fact that you are also an employee, and there might be a contradiction in your ability to be positive in both roles. Even if you're demonstrating effective leadership behaviours, you might still be showing a bit of hypocrisy in how you act as an employee to your own leaders.

The shitty leader, once they become a non-shitty leader, must also face the ramifications and residual leftovers of their past actions; employees may be extremely resistant to these changes. These employees might need to unlearn their own shitty behaviours. As a new and improved active leader, your job is to understand that you had a hand in the employee becoming this way. The next step is to figure out how to bring them into the new paradigm. To do this, you have to be vulnerable, start a dialogue and have new conversations. Work to rebuild trust.

Then again, there will also be the overall shitty employee who, whatever you do, is going to remain the same, regardless. How do you, as a non-shitty leader, who focuses on kind versus right, effectively manage a shitty employee? Is it performance related, or have behavioural choices been made that don't necessarily require performance management? How do you make that call?

You have to empower the employee to understand what their share in this is. They have to buy in. That starts if the leader can own it — acknowledge that their past behaviours played a part. Then engage the employee; "I recognise that you're not ready to fully trust me yet, so let's work out a plan on how we get there."

Remember, shitty leaders are not shitty people. We have collectively created this global epidemic. Now you have the tools to change the face of leadership for the better. Go forward and make it happen. You are able and worthy.

RESOURCES

1. Brown, Brené. 2012 "Listening To Shame." *TED: Ideas Worth Spreading*. Accessed January 14, 2018. Recorded March 2012 at TED2012. https://www.ted.com/talks/Brené_brown_listening_to_shame/

2. Brown, Brené. 2010. "The Power of Vulnerability". *TED: Ideas Worth Spreading*. Accessed January 14, 2018. Recorded June 2010 at TEDxHouston. http://www.ted.com/talks/brene_brown_on_vulnerability

3. Carter, Brandon. 2017. "2017 Employee Engagement & Loyalty Statistics". *Access Perks*, August 28, 2017. https://blog.accessperks.com/2017-employee-engagement-loyalty-statistics

4. Clifton, Jim. 2017. "Workplace Disruption: From Annual Reviews to Coaching". *Gallup*, February 15, 2017. http://news.gallup.com/opinion/chairman/203876/workplace-disruption-annual-reviews-coaching.aspx

5. Earth Unchained. 2014. "Vibrational Frequency: 23 Ways To Raise Your Positive Energy". *Earth Unchained*. Accessed January, 2018.
   http://earthunchained.com/vibrational-frequency/

6. Harter, Jim. 2017. "Dismal Employee Engagement Is a Sign of Global Mismanagement". *Gallup*, December 20, 2017.
   http://news.gallup.com/opinion/gallup/224012/dismal-employee-engagement-sign-global-mismanagement.aspx

7. Harter, Jim & Agrawal, Sangeeta. 2011. "Actively Disengaged Workers and Jobless in Equally Poor Health". *Gallup*, April 20, 2017.
   http://news.gallup.com/poll/147191/Actively-Disengaged-Workers-Jobless-Equally-Poor-Health.aspx

8. Henshaw, Sophie. 2018. "How to Avoid Being Drained by Energy Vampires". *Psych Central*, January 9, 2018.
   https://psychcentral.com/blog/how-to-avoid-being-drained-by-energy-vampires/

9. Rigoni, Brandon & Nelson, Bailey. 2016. "For Millennials, Is Job-Hopping Inevitable?". *Gallup*, November 8, 2016.
   http://news.gallup.com/businessjournal/197234/millennials-job-hopping-inevitable.aspx

10. Robinson, Mark. 2017. *The Ego Continuum: A How-To Guide For Shitty Leaders To Become Less Shitty Through Active Leadership*. Peach Elephant Press. http://www.ego-continuum.co.uk/ego-continuum-book-uk

11. Tedder, Tim. Accessed January 2017. Vulnerability Guide Based on Dr Brené Brown's 2010 TED Talk. http://www.currentscounseling.com/tim-tedder.html

Printed in Poland
by Amazon Fulfillment
Poland Sp. z o.o., Wrocław